DAVENPORT'S
NORTH CAROLINA WILLS AND ESTATE PLANNING LEGAL FORMS

DAVENPORT'S NORTH CAROLINA WILLS AND ESTATE PLANNING LEGAL FORMS

2024 EDITION

written by attorneys
Alex Russell and Robert Maxwell

**SEE BOOKS AND LEGAL FORMS AT
WWW.DAVENPORTPUBLISHING.COM**

COPYRIGHT © 2024 -- ALEX RUSSELL

CREATIVE COMMONS LICENSE. This work is also licensed under a Creative Commons Attribution-NonCommercial-NoDerivatives 4.0 International License.

GOVERNMENT WORKS. No claim is made to copyright or ownership of government materials.

SOME STANDARD FORMS. No copyright or ownership is claimed of "standard" forms or leading forms for the state which are provided in this book, but fair use and privilege to use is claimed. Makers of such forms (often a state agency or hospital) have agreed by word, act, and implication the forms may be used and copied if no profit is sought and no substantial changes made to them. Such makers if not a lawyer or law firm are barred from profit or advantage in practicing law by making forms then limiting use. Forms and other related materials are used here for educational purposes only. Authors strongly believe in a religious duty to help people and do charity.

PUBLICATION DATA
(informal, library may use different data)

Names: Russell, Alex, 1972- author; Maxwell, Robert, 1960- author

Title: Davenport's North Carolina Wills And Estate Planning Legal Forms 2024 Edition

Other Titles: Davenport's Wills

Description: Davenport Publishing 2024

Suggested Identifiers: 9798358369078, LCCN 2021909030, 9798748423373

Subjects: LCSH: Wills--United States;
                  Wills--United States--Forms;
                  Estate Planning--United States;
                  Legal Forms

Classification: LFF KF755 .C55 2024 (or as library chooses)
                  DDC 346.73 Rus--dc24 (or as library chooses)

9 8 7 6 5 4 3 2 1 0 0 0 0 0 2 4

PERMISSION TO COPY AND USE BOOKS FOR FREE

To help people and groups publisher and authors of the book allow mostly free use by giving all a "Creative Commons Attribution-NonCommercial-NoDerivatives 4.0 International License".

Basically, as the image below says, any copying or use is OK if it still shows it is by the authors, is non-commercial (nc) with no price charged, and has no derivatives (nd) so no big changes.

Most users face no limit on copying, using, holding in library to loan out, or giving out copies.

Permission is given to change margins and formatting, do small changes, and cut any blank pages that may occur (but double-check page numbers and table of contents page numbers).

Printing on only 1 side of pages avoids complication of writing on back. Text margins are .75 inches. To do a book not a pamphlet increase left (inside) and decrease right (outside) margins.

Users can design a cover they like but the book title and author names must still appear on it.

Email questions to **davenportpress@gmail.com**.

(This work licensed under a Creative Commons Attribution-NonCommercial-NoDerivatives 4.0 International License.)

FOR FREE COPIES USE WWW.DAVENPORTPUBLISHING.COM OR BUY AT AMAZON.COM.

WARNING

THIS PUBLICATION IS NOT A SUBSTITUTE FOR LEGAL ADVICE. Publisher and authors say and warn this publication is not giving any legal, accounting, or other professional services or advice, which if wanted can be obtained by consulting in person an attorney or some other professional. **No attorney-client relationship or any relationship creating a duty or obligation is agreed to or created by the purchase or use of this publication or forms.**

BOOKS AND FORMS FOR OTHER STATES ARE AVAILABLE. SEE WWW.DAVENPORTPUBLISHING.COM FOR INFORMATION.

CHAPTER	TABLE OF CONTENTS	PAGE NUMBER
CHAPTER 1 – LIST OF FORMS, BOOK BASICS, AND INFORMATION FORM		1
CHAPTER 2 – LEGAL TERMS AND BASIC PROPERTY LAW		6
CHAPTER 3 – WILL BASICS		8
CHAPTER 4 – WILL GIFTS INCLUDING RESIDUE CLAUSE		10
CHAPTER 5 – DEBT, FAMILY, SPOUSE, HOMESTEAD, AND CHILD ISSUES		15
CHAPTER 6 – BASIC IDEAS ABOUT HEALTH CARE FORMS		18

WILL RELATED FORMS

CHAPTER 7 – FORM 1: WILL (STANDARD)		19
CHAPTER 8 – FORM 2: WILL (GUARDIAN)		23
CHAPTER 9 – FORM 3: SELF-PROVING AFFIDAVIT		27
CHAPTER 10 – FORM 4: HANDWRITTEN WILL		29

HEALTH CARE FORMS

CHAPTER 11 – FORM 5: HEALTH CARE POWER OF ATTORNEY		31
CHAPTER 12 – FORM 6: ADVANCE DIRECTIVE FOR A NATURAL DEATH ("LIVING WILL")		38
CHAPTER 13 – FORM 7: DO NOT RESUSCITATE		42

GIVING POWER FORMS

CHAPTER 14 – FORM 8: STATUTORY SHORT FORM POWER OF ATTORNEY		47
CHAPTER 15 – FORM 9: AUTHORIZATION TO CONSENT TO HEALTH CARE FOR MINOR		54
CHAPTER 16 – FORM 10: AUTHORIZATION ABOUT BODILY REMAINS		56

APPENDIX – SAMPLE FILLED OUT LEGAL FORMS		58

CHAPTER 1
LIST OF FORMS, BOOK BASICS, AND INFORMATION FORM

ESTATE PLANNING CONTROLS THINGS IF LATER ABSENT, SICK, OR DEAD

From Davenport Publishing this book covers "Estate Planning", which is a person doing legal documents to control their health care, property, money, children, and funeral if the person is later absent, sick, or dead.

ESTATE PLANNING MOSTLY IS DOING SIMPLE THINGS IN 3 AREAS

Estate Planning is mostly doing simple things in 3 areas: Will Related, Health Care, and Giving Power. This book has many legal forms specially made for North Carolina. Most people use just a few of the forms.

WILL RELATED FORMS

Form 1. Will (Standard) – a Will (also called a "Last Will And Testament") lets a person control things after their death like who gets money and property, who is Executor, and if easier legal options are OK later.

Form 2. Will (Guardian) – this is a Will with a part added to name a person to be Guardian to care for a minor child under 18 if needed (like if both parents later die) and also manage a child's property and money.

Form 3. Self-Proving Affidavit – optional form done with a Will to later help use a Will after a death.

Form 4. Handwritten Will – this Will skips the usual 2 witnesses which saves some work, but all of it must be handwritten by the person doing the Will.

HEALTH CARE FORMS

Form 5. Health Care Power Of Attorney – lets a person name someone to control health care if later needed (like due to a person's later incapacity from inability to talk) and also write health care instructions.

Form 6. Advance Directive For A Natural Death ("Living Will") – this form does serious act of saying stop most health care if later a person is incapacitated and doctors think the health situation is very bad and more health care likely won't help (it is called a Living Will since it applies when a person is still living).

Form 7. Do Not Resuscitate – these are actually 2 forms that do the serious act of immediately refusing most care, and these are short so paramedics can read them fast and they can be used outside any facility.

GIVING POWER FORMS

Form 8. Statutory Short Form Power Of Attorney – lets power over money, property, and other things be shared during a person's life with a trusted person like a spouse, relative, or friend so they can do things.

Form 9. Authorization To Consent To Health Care For Minor – lets a parent share power over a child under 18 with someone so they have power to make decisions about health care and other things if needed.

Form 10. Authorization About Bodily Remains – this form lets instructions be given and if wanted a person be named to control funeral, burial, cremation, ceremonies, and other related matters.

NORTH CAROLINA LAW ON ESTATE PLANNING COVERS MOST PEOPLE HERE

This book is only for North Carolina since Estate Planning laws and legal documents vary among states. North Carolina law applies to Estate Planning usually if a person: a) has their main residence here (their "domicile"), or b) resided here and left but always keeps firm plans to leave any new place (even if a person rents a home elsewhere like some students, military, and workers). Note, many people also do health care forms for the state a health facility they use is in. Most immigrants of any kind can do Estate Planning here.

PERSON HAS POWER TO CONTROL THESE THINGS BUT IT'S OFTEN NOT VITAL

Estate Planning to control health care, property, money, children, funeral, and similar things if a person is absent, sick, or dead is usually easy to do because a person mostly has full power to control these things. Given this usually judges, doctors, and other people mostly just ask: "Based on what a person wrote what did they likely want done?" It is also easy to do because simple legal documents can do the things and simple words can also be used (like listing some property and putting a few names). And despite what many people say often Estate Planning is not worth a lot of effort or money since it often doesn't greatly change the costs, taxes, delays, and later work that is needed. Benefits seem especially low for young people since only 4% of people die by age 50, and only 0.2% of children before age 18 have 2 parents die to need big legal help. Many people spend more energy and money on getting good life insurance to try to help family and friends.

BOOK IS SHORT, QUICKLY SHOWS LEGAL FORMS, AND USES EMPHASIS

This short book may read rough but it can be read fast and it also quickly shows people many legal forms. For emphasis some paragraph titles, boxes, and underlining is used, some small words are skipped, and end quote marks is put before punctuation. Though optional some legal words like Will and Testator are capitalized.

THIS BOOK COVERS THE MAIN LEGAL IDEAS AND SHOULD SUIT MOST PEOPLE

This book covers the main U.S. legal ideas on Estate Planning and big ways North Carolina law is different. This book can't cover all legal issues but should suit most people without some strange situations or wishes. Strange situations or wishes that may need research or a lawyer include: a) strange gift wishes for property and money, b) wealth over $5 million, c) big medical concerns like extreme age, d) property or money going to a person with a disability or special needs, and e) wish to move or hide assets to qualify for government help.

DOCUMENTS MAY NEED TO BE WITNESSED, NOTARIZED, AND USED RIGHT

Some legal documents to be valid need to be "witnessed", which is someone watching the person doing the form sign and then the witness signs it too. Some documents need to be "notarized" where a person who is a "notary" sees it signed and uses an ink stamp and signs too. A person who is a notary (also called a "notary public") are at some banks, brokers, insurance agents, courts, law firms, mail-copy stores, and libraries. Many people first use a phonebook to call for a notary willing to help. The words "subscribe" and "execute" means a person signed a document, and "acknowledgment" means a person said a signature was theirs. If a person signs a document in a foreign language it is usually still binding. In a form the word "respectively" means "in the order just stated". When filling out a form except for signatures the other parts can usually be done in pencil and filled in by anyone. Later people often try to keep the original pages and only hand out copies. Some people have everyone sign multiple copies to have many copies with ink signatures.

FORMS MAKE BINDING LEGAL DOCUMENTS AND BOOK HAS STANDARD FORMS

Legal forms are good at most things involved in Estate Planning and can make binding legal documents. Instead of legal forms a lawyer can be used for Estate Planning but this can be costly, take months of work, and they can make mistakes. In life people often pick a cheaper option. Importantly, often a hospital, charity, state agency, or state legislature has made a form most people use and call the "standard form", and doctors, judges, and other people may not like to follow anything else. This book does provide mostly standard forms.

SOME LESS COMMON OR LESS USEFUL FORMS ARE NOT IN THIS BOOK

This book skips some possible but less common or less useful legal documents.

■ A "Codicil" can modify or add to a Will but it is easier and legally safer to just rewrite the whole Will.

■ Some people do a "Pet Trust" to help a pet, but it's easier to just give money in Will to person given a pet.

■ Some people do a "Revocable Living Trust" so a Trust entity with a Trustee holds property or money during their life, usually done to after death have faster transfer of things and to avoid small delays, costs, or work by others (by "avoiding probate"). But this is rare as it may require moving most of a person's things to a Trust causing maybe years of hassle, mostly to avoid later small work for people happy to be getting things.

■ "Childrens Trust" papers can be done so upon a death a Trust gets things for a minor child to manage till 18, but this is rarely done due to possible costs and hassles and since it rarely matters (as this book explains).

■ Though separate forms exist usually organ donation in handled in drivers license or state ID paperwork.

■ North Carolina law, unlike many states, does not let a list or memo later add small gifts to a Will.

NO FEDERAL, NORTH CAROLINA, OR OTHER TAX IS OWED AT A DEATH

Despite what many people think usually no tax is owed due to a death, including no inheritance, estate, or similar taxes. Most people don't need to worry about these taxes.

The "Federal Estate And Gift Tax" is only owed if a tax credit is used up that covers $13.61 million a person after 2023, and this amount increases each year to adjust for inflation.

At the state and local level there was a North Carolina "Estate Tax" but this was removed by the state legislature years ago, and there no longer is any state or local estate or inheritance tax.

A few states have taxes that may apply for property there if the owner dies, but they usually don't tax things at all if the total is under $3 million or so.

PROBABLY RE-DO DOCUMENTS IF DIVORCE, MARRY, HAVE CHILD, OR MOVE

Divorcing, marrying, having a new child, or moving to a new state can have big legal effects, and if any of these events occur it is recommended people do a new Will and other Estate Planning papers soon. To help most states say a Will from another state is still valid if people move but this is not always certain.

INFORMATION FORM CAN HELP TELL FAMILY AND FRIENDS THINGS

Many people do some kind of "Information Form" so family or friends after a death know helpful things. People can staple financial records and other pages to this. See form on the next pages to use if wanted.

ESTATE PLANNING HELPFUL INFORMATION

For more space attach copies of form or blank pages. Keep pages by Will or other place for Executor or family.

1. Personal Information (Name, Birthdate, Social Security number, special family details, other):

2. Real estate, vehicles, and other major tangible property (especially if people may not find them):

3. Non-tangible assets like stocks, accounts, investments, loans owed you, and business interests:

4. Possible income or insurance like pensions, retirement, disability, insurance, or contracts:

5. Debts owed by you like credit card, loan, student loan, mortgage, car loans, and accounts payable:

6. Names and information of professionals used (attorneys, accountants, brokers, doctors, others):

7. Computer passwords and helpful files, document places, and safes or safe-deposit boxes code/key:

8. Other helpful things, wishes for funeral, special requests, and last messages to family and friends:

CHAPTER 2
LEGAL TERMS AND BASIC PROPERTY LAW

THERE ARE BASIC LEGAL TERMS AND IDEAS IN ESTATE PLANNING

Some legal words and ideas are basic to Estate Planning.

■ "Estate Planning" is about people doing legal documents to control things if later absent, sick, or dead. After a document is done people are mostly free to sell or transfer property, instruct doctors, or change forms.

■ A "person doing a legal document" and "doing a form" means the form is for and affects that person.

■ "Probate" is a legal process to do things after someone's death like transfer property, handle creditors, and authorize a Guardian. Due to changes in the law probate is now often informal, faster, and less costly.

■ A "Will" or "will" (this book uses upper case "W") is a legal document done to control issues after death. The phrase "Last Will And Testament" is used since a "Testament" long ago was a small document done along with a Will to do some things.

■ A person doing a Will is called "Testator" or "Will maker". Before about the year 2000 a woman Testator was called a "Testatrix" and woman Executor called an "Executrix" but this is no longer often said or written.

■ If no valid Will is done a person is "intestate" and then a dead person's property and money is transferred to a spouse, children, and family as intestate law says. <u>Some people a fine with this</u>. This is covered later.

■ A person who died is called the "decedent" or "deceased". A person getting a Will gift is called a "recipient", "beneficiary", or "heir" if related (they "inherit"). "Survive" or "surviving" is to be alive after someone else died. The term "descendants" or "issue" usually means a person's children and grandchildren.

■ A person named in a Will to handle things after someone's death is called an "Executor", but if a judge has to pick someone they are called an "Administrator". <u>The new term "Personal Representative" covers both these things and this new term is now commonly used in Wills in North Carolina and many states</u>.

■ Legally property is: 1) "real property" which is land and buildings ("real estate"), 2) "fixtures" which are things tied to real property (like fences, carpets, and wired-in appliances), or 3) "personal property" which is everything else (like household items, clothes, tools, cars, jewelry, art, moneys, accounts, and stocks),

■ A person under 18 is usually called a "minor" and often a parent or guardian helps them do things. A minor or other person not reasonably able to make wise decisions lacks "capacity" and is "incapacitated".

■ A document giving power to someone is often called a "Power of Attorney" where the "Principal" gives power to someone called the "Agent" or "Attorney-in-Fact" (but they needn't be a real attorney or a lawyer).

■ State law is the "North Carolina General Statutes" and each law is called a "section" or "statute" usually shown by a "s" or a "§" symbol. An example of how to refer to a law is: "N. C. General Statutes § 31-3.4". A legal form found in state law for people to find and use if they want is called a "statutory form".

ESTATE MEANS PROPERTY OF DECEDENT AND ENTITY HOLDING THINGS
The "estate" or "probate estate" means <u>all property and money of a dead person</u> that at death or soon after didn't automatically legally go to new owners. Estate is also the <u>name for a temporary entity run by an Executor to do things after a death</u> (it's like a small corporation, e.g., "Estate of John Alan Smith").

PERSON CAN ONLY GIFT IN WILL WHAT THEY OWN AT DEATH
A person can often only gift by Will things they own at death, <u>so people should research what they own</u>. Basically, by law a person usually owns all they earn as wages and salary, owns their share of income and profit tied to property they own, and owns or partly owns any things their money buys or improves. And for property with "title" documents (real estate or vehicles) or where there is a "listed owner" (like accounts) the named persons are usually the legal owners unless evidence shows special circumstances. If people don't keep track of how much of their money is in an account shared with a spouse, then the account may be seen as jointly owned 50/50. Note, after doing a Will a person can sell stuff, make gifts, or transfer things, so <u>people should consider if they later transferred or lost property they named in a Will gift</u>.

NON-PROBATE TRANSFERS THAT HAPPEN AUTOMATICALLY IGNORE A WILL
It is vital to be aware <u>some money or property of a person who dies may automatically transfer on death</u> or soon after to new owners <u>if certain arrangements were made earlier</u>. This is called "non-probate property". Such things transfer as arranged even if a Will names the same items in some Will gifts.

Examples are: a) a "designated beneficiary" form was done to name people to get an investment or account, b) transfer-on-death accounts were used, and c) real property is held by 2 people as "joint tenants with survivorship" or similar so at a death the surviving person gets things. Also, usually property in a Trust will ignore a Will and transfer as Trust papers say to. Life insurance usually goes to the named beneficiary.

Trying to do non-probate transfers for all things is called "avoiding probate", but few people try this since it can cause years of hassle, benefits are small, and often some thing is missed. <u>When doing a Will people should consider non-probate transfers that will occur automatically at a death and consider what will be left</u>.

THINGS OWNED IN SPECIAL WAYS MAY LIMIT GIFTING IN WILL
A person should consider if they own real estate or other property in special ownership ways which may limit gifting by Will. Laws vary in different states but <u>some common special ways of ownership are</u>:

- "joint tenant with right of survivorship" or similar legal options may be used in papers, so at a death property goes automatically to other named owners despite what a Will says (this is often how spouses hold a home);
- papers say a "life estate" exists, so then if someone dies the other people in papers the get a thing; and
- "Trust property" occurs if paperwork made a Trust entity and then property was transferred into it or this is set to occur, so then the Trust papers control where things put in the Trust go after someone's death.

Simple "joint ownership" with many owners can occur if people do joint papers, all agree to it, buy with joint funds, or if a gift was to many people. Wills <u>can</u> gift joint property, like "I give my half of boat to Ed Hu".

CHAPTER 3
WILL BASICS

A WILL LETS A PERSON CONTROL THINGS AFTER THEIR DEATH

A Will is a legal document done by a person to control some things after their death. A person doing a Will is called the "Testator" or "Will maker". In North Carolina a Testator <u>when signing</u> a Will must be at least age 18, of sound mind (rational with sufficient memory), and not be under duress (unfair pressure or threat).

KEEP SIGNED WILL IN SAFE PLACE IT CAN BE FOUND AFTER A DEATH

A Will should be kept so it can be found within days of a death, like in a desk, drawer, safe, with a person, or (less often) a bank safe deposit box. Family can be told how to find a Will. Also, though rare, people can file a Will at court for safekeeping, and later after a death family or an Executor can withdraw it. N. C. General Statutes § 31-11 (titled "Depositories in offices of clerks of superior court where living persons may file wills").

A WILL USUALLY IS SIGNED WITH 2 WITNESSES

A WILL TO BE VALID USUALLY MUST BE SIGNED WITH 2 WITNESSES

To be a Will words on a page must say or show it is a Will and then a person must <u>sign it in front of at least 2 persons</u> acting as witnesses who then sign too. A Will just spoken on a video or audio recording usually has no legal effect. <u>Some people modify a Will to have 3 or 4 witnesses in case this later helps</u>.

WITNESSES SHOULD BE AT LEAST AGE 18 AND NOT GETTING WILL GIFTS

A person to witness a Will must be at least age 18. Under North Carolina law a Will <u>is</u> still valid if a witness or their spouse are getting gifts in the Will. But normally these gifts to a witness or spouse are void so won't later be done unless somehow there was 2 other proper witnesses not getting any such Will gifts. N. C. General Statutes § 31-10 (titled "Beneficiary competent witness; when interest rendered void").
<u>To avoid these issues most people try to pick witnesses who are "disinterested" which means they or their spouse are not getting Will gifts</u>. It is best but not legally required a witness not be old, live far away, or be named in a Will to be Executor, Guardian, or similar job. Usually witnesses are friends, strangers, or family.

TESTATOR AND 2 WITNESSES SIGN THE WILL WHEN TOGETHER IN 1 ROOM

A person doing a Will usually signs it with 2 or more witnesses who also sign while all are in 1 room and see others sign. A Testator or witness should <u>use their full legal name</u> unless they dislike and rarely use it. People showing others an ID is common but not required. Often witnesses print their name and address. Witnesses only read the 1 paragraph of the Will they will sign. The Testator need not initial the Will pages. Witnesses should be told by someone the document is a Will. Though not required often a Testator says a thing like: "My name is ____ and this is my Will I do voluntarily and ask you 2 people to witness the signing". Some Testators chat a bit with witnesses about a Will to help show they know what they are doing.

MOST WILLS SAY PEOPLE MAY LATER DO INFORMAL PROBATE

Most Wills say after a death the family and friends may do "informal probate" which can avoid costs and delays. Informal probate often is done with just 1 court hearing and often is completed in well under 1 year.

MOST WILLS SAY TO SKIP COSTLY BOND FOR EXECUTOR AND OTHERS

Most Wills helpfully say no "bond" or "surety" is required for any Executor, Guardian, or similar persons. A bond is insurance from a company to insure against misconduct. A Testator usually doesn't want a bond since the persons Testator names are trusted and them later needing a bond will cost the estate money.

CANCELING OLD WILLS IS USUALLY NOT A PROBLEM

So a new Will is followed old Wills should be canceled ("revoked"). To do this a new Will in the first part usually says old Wills are revoked. Or people can revoke a Will by marking it, like with "void" or a giant "X". Usually crossing out just part of a Will has no effect. Revoking a Will usually doesn't bring back an earlier Will.

OFTEN AT START OF A WILL A PERSON NAMES ANY SPOUSE AND CHILDREN

Many Wills start with a place for a Testator to name any current living spouse and children of any age. Natural and adopted children should be put here including any born outside of marriage, but no stepchildren. People without this family can skip this or just write "none". Not doing this may invalidate a Will by indicating a person is mentally unfit, or let a spouse or child not listed ask a judge to give them part or everything by saying a Testator just forgot them. After listing people in a Will a Testator is mostly free to give them nothing.

A WILL NAMES AN EXECUTOR TO DO THINGS AFTER DEATH

A WILL NAMES SOMEONE TO BE EXECUTOR TO DO THINGS AFTER A DEATH

Usually a Will names someone as "Executor" to act after a death. The law gives Executors many helpful legal powers, like to handle debts, find and collect and give new owners property and money, and do probate If a Will fails to name an Executor a judge can pick someone, but family may argue about who to suggest. Note, the term "Personal Representative" and not Executor is now often used in North Carolina for a person doing this job after a death, but these terms mostly mean the same thing. Will gifts can go to an Executor.

EXECUTOR CAN BE PAID AND ESTATE PAYS FOR EXECUTOR'S EXPENSES

North Carolina law says an Executor can ask to can be paid and usually get paid for the hours of work spent, but unlike some states there is not a right to get a percent of money and property. For example, an Executor spending 5 hours a week for 40 weeks might ask for $40 an hour and so ask to get paid $8000. But often Executors later skip asking for pay so as to not owe income tax and leave more resources to carry out more Will gifts. Costs any Executor has like for insurance, utilities, repairs, funeral, mortgage, security, accountants, attorneys, and probate costs are paid for with some money or property of a decedent's estate. Any lawyer hired is paid what they and Executor agree on which may be an hourly rate or a fixed sum.

EXECUTOR MUST BE AT LEAST 18 AND SECOND PERSON RARELY IS NEEDED

A person to be Executor must be at least age 18 and have no felony criminal record. Later a judge may later block a person who seems too unsuitable. A person to be Executor needn't live in the state if they pick a local person or lawyer to get mail. Naming 2 people to be Executor at the same time is rare due to risk of arguments or delays, and since any 1 person named is trusted. People can name a 2nd fallback person to be Executor if needed but most skip this because it is rarely needed and a judge can always pick someone. To add such a 2nd person a Will can say: "or if they're reasonably unable to serve I name _____ to serve".

CHAPTER 4
WILL GIFTS INCLUDING RESIDUE CLAUSE

MAIN USE OF A WILL IS TO WRITE GIFTS TO HAPPEN AFTER DEATH

Most people use a Will mainly to legally say what happens to their property and money after their death, usually by writing down various Will gifts to occur when they die. Verbal and even writings about this are not usually valid if not in a written Will. A Will can control property acquired after it was signed. The end of this chapter covers "intestate law" which says where a person's things go at death if no valid Will handles this.

GIFTING IN A WILL USING SIMPLE WORDS OFTEN IS BEST

Making gifts in a Will using simple words is often best, using words like "I give to" and "I gift to". This is legally fine and avoids confusing legal words like "bequest", "devise", and "legacy" which few people know.

A PERSON IS MOSTLY FREE TO GIFT THEIR THINGS AS WANTED

A person is mostly free to give at death their money and property as they want. But creditors a decedent owed money, a spouse, and minor children under age 18 may have some rights which this book later covers.

IN WILL CAN DO SPECIFIC GIFTS TO GIFT PARTICULAR PROPERTY

Most Wills have "specific gifts" to gift _particular things_. Specific gifts can be any property, like "I give boat to Ed Blom" and "I give UBank account #84553873 to Sue Wu". If a gift is not clear the law assumes all of a kind of thing is given, like "I give jewelry to Ann Po" means _all_ jewelry. But gifting specific property can have surprises like value of items can change, or a Will gift may later fail to occur if property is not owned at death.

IN WILL CAN DO GENERAL GIFTS LIKE OF MONEY

Wills can do "general gifts" where what is gifted is not particular property but can be flexibly chosen, like "I give 1 of my 3 cars to Ed Po" which lets an Executor pick which car. The usual general gift is money, like "I give $5 to Ed Hu". Money gifts are easy to write, let equal gifts be made, and are legally safer for many reasons. To carry out money gifts an Executor usually uses accounts or sells some property in the estate.

PERSON IN WILL GIFT USUALLY MUST SURVIVE OR GIFT DOES NOT OCCUR

Many Wills like this book's Will forms say a person named in a Will gift must survive (live past) the Testator for the gift to occur unless gift language specifically says different. If survival is not required for a Will gift then what happens if a person named in a Will gift later dies before Testator can be legally unclear. People doing a Will should consider how Will gifts to people dying before Testator usually have no effect. People if they see a person in a Will gift has died can re-do a Will or just let the Residue Clause handle it.

RESIDUE CLAUSE IS CATCH-ALL THAT HELPFULLY GIFTS ANYTHING LEFT

This chapter later covers how a Residue Clause in Will gifts property or money not already gifted or used.

LATER DIVORCE OR MURDER CANCELS WILL GIFTS TO THE ACTING PERSON

If a person divorces or murders a Testator then by state law usually all Will gifts to them are cancelled.

GIFTS IN WILL CAN GO TO A GROUP OR CLASS OF PEOPLE
To save work a Will gift can go to a group or class of people like certain family <u>if who is meant is later easy to determine</u>. People can say roughly how <u>much in total</u> is gifted to be clearer. Examples are: "I give $10 to each person in my 2018 bowling team" and "I give $10 to each of my grandkids so this is about $100 in total."

IF PERSON DIES A WILL GIFT CAN GO TO LINEAL DESCENDANTS PER STIRPES
A Will gift can say it goes to a person but if they don't survive then to their "lineal descendants per stirpes". <u>Descendants are a person's children and grandchildren</u>. "Per stirpes" means "by branch" and is about how to spread property and money, and it mostly tries to divide things so <u>each family branch gets an equal share</u>. Most Wills use "lineal descendants" language in a Residue Clause. <u>An example shows how it works</u>:

A Will may say: **"Clothes to Sue Wu but if they don't survive to their lineal descendants per stirpes"**, and this means if Sue Wu has died and her son Ken Wu is living and her other son Ben Wu has died but left 2 children then, legally, by law Ken Wu himself gets 50% and Ben Wu's 2 children each get 25%.

GIFT RECIPIENTS DYING BEFORE TESTATOR IS RARE AND EASY TO HANDLE
Having a person named in a Will gift die is rare and usually noticed and then <u>people often re-do a Will to replace any dead person in Will gifts</u>, or some people don't act and trust a Residue Clause to handle it.

PEOPLE CAN ADD AN ALTERNATE BENEFICIARY LIKE FOR SPECIAL ITEMS
Some people for the small risk a recipient in a Will gift dies before a Testator, and maybe for special items, <u>write a bit to add an "alternate beneficiary"</u>, like "I give boat to Ed Fox but if they don't survive me to Ann Fox".

GIFT BENEFICIARIES CAN GET PERCENTAGE RATHER THAN EQUAL SHARE
If a Will gift goes to multiple people the law assumes equal shares, but if wanted percentages can be used to make unequal gifts, like "I give boat 90% to John Smith and 10% to Mary Baker".

PROPERTY OR MONEY IN A JOINT GIFT GOES TO MULTIPLE PEOPLE
The same property or money can go to many people to each get a part, and this is called a "joint gift". For example, "I give boat and all hats to Ann Baxter and Mary Ann Swanson" means each person owns part of every item. People later can split things by agreement or an Executor can decide how to divide items. If a person in a joint gift has died their part usually is left to transfer under a Residue Clause.

AFTER A DEATH FAMILIES OFTEN LET PEOPLE TAKE ITEMS UNOFFICIALLY
Many families let people take items <u>unofficially</u> in ways a person said, wrote on notes, or showed by stickers. If anyone officially objects a judge will have a Will and law be followed, but later people can voluntarily retransfer items. Note, North Carolina unlike some states does not let a short list or memo add small gifts to a Will.

CAN LEAVE SOME WILL GIFT AREAS BLANK OR WRITE TO SAY SKIP GIFTS
A person can choose to not use some gifts areas in a Will legal form, like by just leaving areas blank, writing things like "SKIPPED" or "NONE", or using a computer to delete some gift lines. Judges and others usually do not care about neatness or empty spaces in Wills, and will follow whatever parts are filled in.

RESIDUE CLAUSE GIFTING ANYTHING LEFT IS MAIN WAY TO GIFT THINGS

THE RESIDUE CLAUSE IS A CATCH-ALL THAT GIFTS ANYTHING LEFT

Most Wills by the end have a Residue Clause to give property or money left in a person's estate not gifted earlier in a Will or used other ways. All that is left this way is called the "Residue". Many people let this clause handle most things. This avoids all need to list and describe property and money and also has less legal risk.

USUAL RESIDUE CLAUSE HAS 2 PARTS

A short 2 part Residue Clause is usual and is used in this book's Will forms, and it has:

1) a 1st space to name persons to get things if they survive the Testator (many name a spouse or closest family here), and if several people are named here but only some survive the survivors split things, and

2) a 2nd space to name persons to get things if all in the 1st space don't survive (many people name next closest family or friends here), and if a person in the 2nd space has died their descendants get their share.

EXAMPLE OF 2 PART RESIDUE CLAUSE:

"RESIDUE CLAUSE: The rest, residue, and remainder of my estate, and anything else, I give to:

a) to ____Jay Doe my husband_____ who survive me and with persons just named who survive me taking the share of non-survivors, then if anything remains

b) to ____Sam Doe, Ann Wu, and Pam Ax_____ and if any of those just named do not survive me their part goes to their lineal descendants per stirpes."

In this example things may go to "descendants" so to a person's children and grandchildren, and things may be divided "per stirpes" which means equal among family branches. In this example if Jay Doe has survived he gets everything. If he has died and also Sam Doe hasn't survived but he left 2 children then, legally, Sam's 2 children split the 1/3 share of his (so get 1/6 each) and the other 2 persons in 2nd part (Ann Wu and Pam Ax) get 1/3 each. Usually the first people named in the clause won't die so gets things.

SOME PEOPLE USE PERCENTAGES TO GIFT DIFFERENT AMOUNTS OF RESIDUE

Some people use percentages in a Residue Clause to get the exact split wanted. This can gift a lot (like to a person's children) and gift a small bit (like to a grandchild or more distant people). *See example in Appendix.*

SOME PEOPLE WRITE THE SAME THING IN BOTH PARTS OR SKIP A PART

Some people put the same names in both clause spaces or skip part of it to do certain things. For example, a person with no spouse may skip the 1st part and in 2nd part name their children (including any who died who had kids of their own) so all branches of a person's descendants get a share. *See example in Appendix.*

SOME PEOPLE CHANGE A RESIDUE CLAUSE TO HAVE 1 PART

Some people change a Residue Clause to have just 1 part since this can gift more equally and be easier to understand. *See example in Appendix.* For example a Residue Clause can be made to say:

"The rest, residue, and remainder of my estate, and anything else, I give to: _____ who survive me and if any of those just named do not survive me their part goes to their lineal descendants per stirpes."

MUST SUFFICIENTLY DESCRIBE NAMES AND PROPERTY IN A WILL

PUTTING NAMES OF PEOPLE OR GROUPS IN A WILL IS FAIRLY EASY

Putting names in a Will is fairly easy. <u>Later a judge or Executor assume a person putting names in a Will meant to gift to people they know, so common names are OK unless 2 friends or family use the same name</u>. Details can help if names won't be recognized or to be friendly, like "I give $5 to my nurse Sue Smith" and "I give $5 to loyal pal Ed Dutton". If people mostly used a nickname "also known as" or "a/k/a" may help, like "I give $5 to Dan Smith a/k/a Big Red". Gifts can go to a charity, a government, or a group, like "I give $8 to Goodwill Charities, "I give $8 to the Boston Public Library, Boston, MA", and "I give $8 to Holy Trinity Church of Dallas, Texas". People sometimes phone to learn a charity's or organization's official name.

PUTTING DESCRIPTIONS OF ITEMS IN WILL GIFTS IS FAIRLY EASY

Describing items in gifts is fairly easy. <u>Later a judge or Executor assume a person in a Will meant to gift items they own, and rarely do people own similar things so there is later confusion</u>. Often OK is doing gifts with simple words like: "I give ax to Ed Wu" and "I give big table to Jed Fox". It's OK to gift by category or a list, like: "I give tools to Sam Lee" and "I give cow, van, and harp to Sue Po". For financial items plain words can be used, like "I give bank accounts and stocks to Ann Bima", or details can be used, like: "I give Wells Fargo bank account ending 8714 to Tom Hud". <u>Gifting using a location is riskier</u> as judges will ignore a Will gift if it seems items were placed to affect gifting and for no "independently significant" life reason. So, "I give Ed Po items in my desk and safe" a judge might not follow, but "I give Ed Po hats at cabin" likely is OK.

DESCRIBING REAL PROPERTY IS HARD IF NOT USING RESIDUE OR TITLE

Gifting real property (real estate) and fixtures (things tied to real property like fences, furnaces, and wiring) at death can be hard to do right and the legally safer way to do this is:

a) <u>do nothing specific so it's handled by a Will residue clause</u>, or b) <u>have a lawyer or other person put names in a deed or other document for the real property</u> so then named persons legally get it when the owner dies.

Gifting real property at death a few other ways is legally harder. Helpfully a gift of real property <u>using a location</u> by law gifts <u>all land, buildings, and fixtures located there</u> with no need to list out what's there.

It is possible to <u>gift real property at a particular address with very plain words</u>, like a house, fixtures, and land can be fully given by something like: "I give 86 Maxwell Street, Raleigh, North Carolina, to Sue Ann Brown".

People can do a <u>blanket gift</u> giving all of a kind of property, like, "I give all real property and fixtures in Wake County, North Carolina to Ann Ivy Hill " or "I give all real property and fixtures of mine to Eric Paul Carlson".

Giving real property in a Will using a "legal description" is how some lawyers do it, but this can be hard to do. If using a legal description people must write without mistakes <u>the full legal description of maybe many lines</u> into a Will with no abbreviation at all. A legal description might be found on a deed or on mortgage papers. Legal descriptions may refer to a "lot" or "blocks" on a map which is recorded in land records of a county, or it may refer to a path around the land borders with various angles, distances, and iron stakes.

CONDITIONS ON WILL GIFTS ARE RARE DUE TO POSSIBLE PROBLEMS
Putting conditions on a gift, like "I give Ann Poe $90 if she graduates college", can cause problems like years of delay, risk of lawsuits, and big attorney's fees. Due to all this conditions are rarely put on Will gifts.

MOST STATES AND WILLS SAY PEOPLE TO GET GIFTS MUST SURVIVE 5 DAYS
Helpful laws in most states and all this book's Will forms say if a person dies within 5 days (120 hours) of a Testator or simultaneously, then they are legally seen as dying before the Testator. This skips the need to prove exact time of death (like if people die in 1 accident), and avoids a Will gift or right to something going to someone who then soon dies within days (so an item may have to go through multiple probate proceedings).

MOST WILLS HAVE A MISCELLANEOUS PART WITH HELPFUL LANGUAGE
Most Wills have a "Miscellaneous" page with legal language that might help avoid later legal problems.

INTESTATE LAW COVERS PROPERTY OR MONEY NOT HANDLED BY WILL

INTESTATE LAW CONTROLS THINGS NOT HANDLED BY A WILL

State "intestate law" says <u>if a person dies with no valid Will</u> or <u>if anything is left after Will and all transfers are done</u> then certain surviving (living) family of the dead person get property and money left in their estate. Some people like what intestate law says and choose to skip a Will, but often doing a Will has some benefit. If somehow property or money is left after following intestate law then it goes to the state of North Carolina. Note, "descendants" and "issue" both mean a person's children and grandchildren, and if someone dies who would've get an intestate share often their descendants get that share. In many states the law often says half and sometimes all goes to any surviving spouse (if any), then half or any remainder goes to decedent's children (or if dead their own child gets that share), and then next closest family. In intestate law a legally adopted child counts but not usually a foster-child or step-child.

North Carolina intestate law can be simple, and <u>if a person dies with living descendants like children but no spouse then some descendants get everything</u>, or <u>if a person dies with living spouse but no descendants or parents then the spouse gets everything</u>. But in other family situations the law can be complex, like with some minimum amount going to any spouse and various splitting of rest between other family members. For exact information people may want to look up the law, like N. C. General Statutes § 29-14 (titled "Share of surviving spouse") and N. C. General Statutes § 29-15 (titled "Shares of others than surviving spouse").

CHAPTER 5
DEBT, FAMILY, SPOUSE, HOMESTEAD, AND CHILD ISSUES

THIS CHAPTER COVERS CERTAIN ISSUES THAT SOME PEOPLE CAN SKIP
This chapter covers debt, family, spouse, homestead, and child issues, and some people can skip parts.

DEBT ISSUES

PAYING DECEDENT'S DEBTS MAY USE UP RESOURCES AND REDUCE GIFTS
If a decedent had debts then creditors owed may ask a judge to be paid from decedent's money or property before Will gifts and certain transfers occur. How debts are paid is set by state law and a Will need not describe this. Funds to pay debts comes from decedent's money and property so may affect (in order) the Will Residue, Will general gifts, Will specific gifts, and non-probate transfers. Probate, health care, taxes, and funeral costs by law have some priority to be paid first. For certain reasons often not all debts are paid. People should consider how paying debts may use up money or property, leaving less to carry out Will gifts. A spouse and family usually aren't liable for decedent's debts unless they actually guaranteed or co-signed.

SECURED DEBTS LIKE MORTGAGE OR VEHICLE LIEN ARE NOT PAID OFF
Laws in most states say do not pay off any secured debts on property of a decedent like a house mortgage or vehicle lien even if other debts are paid by Executor or in probate. This avoids using up estate resources on paying these usually big debts. Due to this, all this book's Will forms say to not usually pay off any secured debts. But if a Testator wants they can 1) put in a Will an order to pay (like, "Executor pay off the house mortgage"), or 2) gift ample enough money to pay off a secured debt to the person getting the property. Most banks let the new owners after a death keep paying monthly any secured debt like a mortgage or lien.

FAMILY ISSUES

FAMILY RIGHTS MAY BE USED TO GET FAMILY THINGS BEFORE DEBTS
Many states have "Family Rights" a decedent's surviving spouse or young children can use, and this may helpfully let them get things even before most debts of decedent are paid and before Will gifts are carried out. State law varies but this can include an "Exempt Property" right to some of decedent's household items and vehicles to use to live, like $20,000 of this. This can include a "Family Allowance" right to get some money to live on for a year or so from the decedent's property and money. See N.C. General Statutes § 30-15, titled "When spouse entitled to [$60,000] allowance". This can include the right to use a "Small Estate Affidavit" to quickly get a spouse or children most things if a decedent didn't leave much, like under $50,000 of things. North Carolina law partly has these rights, and most people with a spouse or children accept they have rights to get some things. So family don't cause legal trouble by using these rights often a person in some way gives over 50% and any owned family dwelling to any spouse or small children. People if wanted can do research.

SPOUSE ISSUES

NORTH CAROLINA USES SEPARATE PROPERTY LAW FOR SPOUSES

North Carolina like most states not in Western U.S. uses the Separate Property Law system that says any married person mostly owns their money and property separately and not jointly shared with a spouse. Due to this a married person here is often free to sell during life or gift by Will most their property and money and not involve a spouse. Mainly in West U.S. are 9 states that use the complex Community Property Law system (Arizona, California, Louisiana, Idaho, Nevada, New Mexico, Texas, Washington, and Wisconsin). This system says property or money is owned 50/50 by spouses as Community Property if it comes any work while married (like wages or salary) or if items are bought or improved with other Community Property. But joint ownership by 2 spouses and not separate ownership can arise in other ways, like by agreement, both spouses paying part of the purchase price, if a gift was to both spouses, or if paperwork calls it joint.

SPOUSE CAN GET ELECTIVE SHARE INSTEAD OF FOLLOWING WILL

In most states a spouse if unhappy with what a Will and other transfers may give them has a right to instead choose (elect) an "Elective Share" of a share of a dead spouse's property and money rather than get what a Will says. States have the Elective Share to be fair to a spouse. To avoid this spouses need to sign a pre-nuptial or similar agreement by a lawyer which is rare. In North Carolina the Elective Share is 15% to start, 25% after 5 years of marriage, 33% after 10 years of marriage, and is 50% after 15 years of marriage. N. C. General Statutes § 30-3.1. In North Carolina in some cases this can cover property or money a decedent gave away or, also, even things not in the estate. Clearly if a spouse uses an Elective Share this may take so much it may interfere with transfers to other people. Overall, to avoid a spouse wanting to use the Elective Share or other rights of a spouse almost all married people give over 1/2 of things to any spouse.

HOMESTEAD ISSUES

In many states a surviving spouse or minor children have some right to get (or just stay in for years) the house or mobile home the family lives in and owned by a decedent under a "Homestead Law". North Carolina law partly has these rights, and most people with a spouse or children accept they may have some rights to get or stay. N. C. General Statutes § 29-30 (titled: "Election of surviving spouse to take life interest in lieu of intestate share provided"). So family don't cause legal trouble by wanting to use these rights usually a person by Will or other way gives over 50% and any main family house to any spouse or small children.

CHILD ISSUES

WILL CAN NAME A GUARDIAN OF THE PERSON TO CARE FOR YOUNG CHILD

If a parent dies with a child under age 18 then any other natural or adopted parent (but not a step-parent) almost always automatically gets control of the child's care (including health care, school, and home issues). This won't occur only if the other parent will be unavailable a long time or is proven unfit in court which is rare. But just in case it is later needed (like later both parents die) a Will often names a healthy and willing relative or friend as "Guardian Of The Person" to if needed give this care for a child. Some states use other names.

WILL CAN NAME A GUARDIAN OF THE ESTATE TO MANAGE CHILD'S PROPERTY

Since a child until age 18 can't legally easily control property including money a Will often names a person to be "Guardian Of The Estate" to have the job of managing a young child's property and money. Many states call this a Conservator. This person decides each year how to use property and money on a child's needs (like on school, health care, and living costs) and then usually at age 18 anything left then goes to the child. A person paying things for a child can ask to be paid back. A judge often holds a yearly hearing to review all spending. As a nice 2nd option to avoid work and costs most Wills say an Executor may name a person including themselves as "Custodian" to manage things under the new Uniform Transfers To Minors Act.

MOST WILLS NAME 1 PERSON TO CARE FOR CHILD AND THEIR PROPERTY

This book's Will forms and most parents name the same 1 person to care for a child and also manage a child's property and money. In North Carolina if 1 person does both jobs they are also a "General Guardian". People can change a Will to name different people for the 2 positions, but this is rarely worth the legal hassle and mental effort since parents dying is rare, rarely do children get much, a person smart enough to handle a child often can handle money, and naming different people can lead to arguments and maybe costly lawsuits. Will gifts can go to someone named in a Will to be a Guardian.

PERSON TO HELP A CHILD MUST BE AT LEAST 18

To act in these positions a person must be at least 18 and not be convicted of a felony crime anywhere. A person need not be a resident of North Carolina if they name someone local (like a lawyer) to get mail. A judge may also later block a person who seems too unsuitable. The choice by the last living parent is usually followed. If no Will names a person for a position or they're unavailable a judge can pick someone, but family may argue between themselves on who to suggest. Naming 2 people to act at the same time in the same position is rare since 2 persons may argue and any 1 person named is often smart enough to act alone. Sometimes the 2 people in a married couple are named for the same position but there can be problems if they divorce or fight. Some Wills add a 2nd person to serve if the 1st person named is later not available, like: "or if they are later unable to serve I name _____ to serve"). But most people skip naming a fallback person since it is rarely needed, if a problem is seen a Will can be redone by a person, or a judge can just pick.

NAMING PERSONS TO HELP CHILD RARELY MATTERS

A child under 18 having parents die is rare so parents shouldn't worry much about naming people to help. A good U.S. study looked at 72,240 people under age 18 and found only 2014 had lost 1 parent (so 2.78%) and only 97 had lost 2 parents (so a very small 0.13%). *Parent Mortality Census SIPP Paper #288.*

CHAPTER 6
BASIC IDEAS ABOUT HEALTH CARE FORMS

BASIC IDEAS HELP PEOPLE UNDERSTAND CONTROLLING HEALTH CARE

Some ideas help people understand health care forms.

■ By law people controls their own health care by telling medical personnel what they want <u>unless they are "incapacitated"</u> by insufficient ability to a) <u>communicate</u> verbally or by notes, b) be <u>rational</u>, or c) be <u>conscious</u>. Most people keep control of their own care till death or till no big treatment options remain, but some people worry they may be incapacitated a long time so want to do health care forms.

■ Legal documents that help control health care are usually called "Advanced Directives".

■ If an adult 18 or older becomes incapacitated <u>the adult's closest family like spouse or adult child usually can make emergency decisions</u>. But later they usually must then rush to a judge to get further power if no legal document gives them more power over health care.

■ In legal documents a <u>person can be named to have control of health care</u> if needed. This person is often called the "Health Care Agent" or similar.

■ In legal documents people can give <u>written medical instructions that doctors, family, and Agent must obey</u>.

■ Parents even without legal documents usually have power over health care of <u>children under age 18</u>.

■ Some <u>married people</u> do documents to give a spouse power over medical care if they are incapacitated. Some adults give this power to parents. Young people are rarely badly sick so often skip doing these things.

■ Pain relief like pain drugs or comfort care is still given even if documents say to stop or limit other care.

■ <u>Most people only do 1 legal document</u> about health care that often names someone to control health care if needed and has a spot for basic instructions (this is sometimes called a "Health Care Power of Attorney").

■ For the rare times stopping health care seems more likely to matter (like due to extreme illness or old age):

-- most people do nothing special and trust family or Health Care Agent to wisely decide when to stop care (they can weigh many factors like pain, cost, likely difficulty of treatment, beliefs, and chances of recovery);

-- a few people do a serious document to say to stop most health care if <u>later</u> doctors think an incapacitated person has very bad health and more medical care likely won't help (sometimes this is called a "Living Will";

-- a few people do a serious document to say <u>starting immediately</u> to not try most medical care (sometimes this is called a "Do-Not-Resuscitate" if about resuscitation or called a "Physician's Order" if about many treatments).

CHAPTER 7
FORM 1: WILL (STANDARD)

FORM 1 IS A STANDARD WILL THAT IS FLEXIBLE BUT WITHOUT GUARDIANS

Form 1 is a flexible Will that lets a person control many things after their death. This form has no part about a Guardian so is for a person with no child under age 18. A person doing a Will is called a Testator.

THIS FORM IS A WILL WITH SEVERAL PARTS

The form starts with lines for a person to put their name (a full legal name is best but not required) and place of main residence (most put a county but some put a city). The Will is still valid if people later move.

Paragraph 1, "Living Spouse And Children", is used to write names of any living spouse and living children (but not step-children) of any age (or if there are none skip this or maybe put "none"). This helps show a person is mentally fit enough to do a Will. Wrongly not listing someone may cause legal problems.

Paragraph 2, "Gifts", has many spaces to make some specific gifts of particular property or some general gifts like of money. People can delete, copy and paste to add more, or leave blank these gift lines.

Paragraph 3, "Residue", has a Residue Clause to say any property and money left after earlier Will parts and other transfers is to be distributed in the way a person wrote in the blank parts of this paragraph.

Paragraph 4, "Administration", names a person to be Personal Representative to do things after a person's death (in the past the term Executor was usually used in North Carolina for the person doing this).

Paragraph 5, "Miscellaneous", has paragraphs of legal language to help avoid certain legal issues.

Last is a paragraph for Testator to put the date and sign, and a paragraph for 2 witnesses to put the date, sign, and print the addresses they live at.

USUAL RESIDUE CLAUSE HAS 2 PLACES TO NAME PERSONS TO GET THINGS

In a Will "Residue Clause" anything left over after other Will parts is transferred as the clause directs. Many people use a Residue Clause to gift most their things. In this Will form's Residue Clause there is:

1) a 1st space to name 1 or more persons to get the Residue, and if any named here have died before the Will maker then other persons named here in this 1st space take the dead person's share, and

2) a 2nd space to name people to get things if all people named in the 1st space have died, and if any people named in the 2nd space have died their shares go to "lineal descendants" like their children.

People often put in the 1st space a spouse or closest family or friends, and in 2nd space next closest people.

TESTATOR AND 2 WITNESSES WHILE TOGETHER SIGN WILL

This Will after being filled out (except bits intentionally left blank) must be signed by the person doing the Will (the "Testator") in front of at least 2 persons acting as witnesses at least age 18 who then also sign.

LAST WILL AND TESTAMENT

I, _____, of _____, North Carolina, do revoke all prior Wills and testamentary documents and do make, publish, and declare this as my Will. I am of sound mind and under no duress or undue influence and act voluntarily.

1. LIVING SPOUSE AND CHILDREN. To show I am mentally fit and have sufficient memory to do a Will I do say I now have the following living spouse and living children: _____
_____.

2. GIFTS. I give these gifts in this Will, but to get a gift in this section the recipient must survive me except as otherwise stated below.

I give _____ to _____.
I give _____ to _____.
I give _____ to _____.
I give _____ to _____.
I give _____ to _____.
I give _____ to _____.
I give _____ to _____.
I give _____ to _____.
I give _____ to _____.
I give _____ to _____.
I give _____ to _____.
I give _____ to _____.

3. RESIDUE. The rest, residue, and remainder of my estate, and anything else, I give:
   a) to _____ who survive me, and with persons just named who survive me taking the share of non-survivors, then if anything remains
   b) to _____ and if any of those just now named do not survive me their part goes to their lineal descendants per stirpes.

4. ADMINISTRATION. I name, nominate, and appoint _____
as Personal Representative including for me, my Will, and my estate.

5. MISCELLANEOUS. The following applies to this Will and generally.
    In this Will no part left unfilled is a mistake including spaces in the residue clause.
    The facts support and I want North Carolina law to apply to this Will and my estate.
    I order that my just debts, funeral and related expenses, and taxes be paid as soon after my death as practical but only those items my Personal Representative chooses to pay.
    Priority of Will gifts of the same type is based on the order they are made in this Will.
    The words give and gift also means a devise, bequest, grant, legacy, or similar.
    I am intentionally not providing by Will or other ways for some family, including I am not providing for some children of mine and also children of a deceased child of mine.
    If a Will gift reasonably mentions survival then survival is an absolute condition and anti-lapse laws or similar provisions have no effect and without survival the gift lapses. Unless a Will gift specifies otherwise if a Will gift goes to multiple recipients if any do not survive me the part to them lapses and instead goes to other surviving recipients.
    No earlier transfer reduces a Will gift unless I usually called it a loan or advancement.
    In this Will any gendered word includes all genders, and the singular includes the plural and vice versa, and they can mean a single person or many persons.
    Unless a Will specifically says otherwise a secured debt including a mortgage or lien shall not be paid off including by a Personal Representative or in probate, and a recipient of a Will gift of property takes it subject to debts. Also, no recipient of property who may lose it or who pays to keep it may have my estate or others pay or do exoneration.
    If I somehow lost ownership of an item in a specific Will gift the gift is extinguished.
    I request and authorize any informal, summary, and quick probate or similar action. Any Personal Representative may act independently with no supervision of any court, including independent administration, and with no inventory, appraisal, or other action.
    I give any Personal Representative the a) fullest authority, discretion, and powers allowed by state law, b) power to lease, sell, mortgage, convey, or keep property including real property in a manner and time they deem helpful or proper, and c) authority to settle or pay claims or debts in the time and manner they choose. Any Personal Representative or other fiduciary shall have all powers and authorities that may be given by statute or common law in any jurisdiction they may act, including under North Carolina law.
    Any Guardian of any type, Conservator, Custodian, or other person managing a minor's property or money may use or invade the principal and sell property without court action.
    If context permits the terms Personal Representative and Executor and Administrator are interchangeable, Conservator and Guardian of the Estate and Guardian of Property and Custodian are interchangeable, and residue and residuary are interchangeable. Any such person may stand in the place of and have all powers like the others named here.

The residue includes lapsed or failed gifts, insurance paid to the estate, digital assets, inheritances owed me, and all I had power of appointment or testamentary disposition over.

Any Personal Representative may access, manage, delete, modify, transfer, and otherwise control any digital accounts and assets I had any interest in or power over.

Any Personal Representative, Executor, Administrator, Guardian of any type like for a person or estate, Conservator, Custodian, and any other fiduciary under this Will or otherwise shall qualify and serve without bond, surety, security, surety bond, or similar.

If evidence does not show it likely a person survived me by 120 hours (5 days) then for this Will and my estate they shall be deemed in all ways as having died before me.

If part of this Will is by law invalid or unenforceable other provisions remain in effect.

Any Personal Representative may at any time transfer money or property of a minor under age 18 to a Custodian to act under the North Carolina Uniform Transfers to Minors Act or similar law anywhere, and may pick a person to be Custodian including themselves.

TESTATOR

IN WITNESS WHEREOF, I, _____, the Testator, sign my name to this instrument this, and do hereby declare that I sign and execute this instrument as my Will and that I sign it willingly, that I execute it as my free and voluntary act for the purposes therein expressed, and that I am 18 years of age or older, of sound mind, and under no constraint or undue influence.

_____
Signature of Testator

WITNESSES

We, _____ and _____, the Witnesses, sign our names to this instrument, and do hereby declare that the Testator signs and executes this instrument as the Will of the Testator in our presence and that the Testator signs it willingly, and that each of us at the request of the Testator and in the presence and hearing of the Testator, and in the presence and hearing of each other, hereby signs this Will to function legally as witness to the Testator's signing, and to the best of our knowledge the Testator is eighteen years of age or older, of sound mind, and under no constraint or undue influence.

_____ _____
Signature of Witness #1   Address of Witness #1

_____ _____
Signature of Witness #2   Address of Witness #2

CHAPTER 8
FORM 2: WILL (GUARDIAN)

FORM 2 IS A WILL WITH GUARDIAN PART FOR PEOPLE WITH YOUNG CHILD
Form 2 is a Will with a Guardian part to be used by a person with a minor child under age 18.

FORM IS A WILL WITH SEVERAL PARTS INCLUDING A GUARDIAN PART
The form starts with lines for a person to put their name (a full legal name is best but not required) and place of main residence (most put a county but some put a city). The Will is still valid if people later move.

Paragraph 1, "Living Spouse And Children", is used to write names of any living spouse and living children (but not step-children) of any age (or if there are none skip this or maybe put "none"). This helps show a person is mentally fit enough to do a Will. Wrongly not listing someone may cause legal problems.

Paragraph 2, "Gifts", has many spaces to make some specific gifts of particular property or some general gifts like of money. People can delete, copy and paste to add more, or leave blank these gift lines.

Paragraph 3, "Residue", has a Residue Clause to say any property and money left after earlier Will parts and other transfers is to be distributed in the way a person wrote in the blank parts of this paragraph.

Paragraph 4, "Administration", names a person to be Personal Representative to do things after a person's death (in the past the term Executor was usually used in North Carolina for the person doing this).

<u>**Paragraph 5, "Guardian"**, names a person to care for minor children under age 18 if needed (like if both parents die) and also a person to manage property and money of children.</u>

Paragraph 6, "Miscellaneous", has paragraphs of legal language to help avoid certain legal issues.

Last is a paragraph for Testator to put the date and sign, and a paragraph for 2 witnesses to put the date, sign, and print the addresses they live at.

USUAL RESIDUE CLAUSE HAS 2 PLACES TO NAME PERSONS TO GET THINGS
In a Will "Residue Clause" anything left over after other Will parts is transferred as the clause directs. Many people use a Residue Clause to gift most their things. In this Will form's Residue Clause there is:

1) a 1st space to name 1 or more persons to get the Residue, and if any named here have died before the Will maker then other persons named here in this 1st space take the dead person's share, and

2) a 2nd space to name people to get things if all people named in the 1st space have died, and if any people named in the 2nd space have died their shares go to "lineal descendants" like their children.

People often put in the 1st space a spouse or closest family or friends, and in 2nd space next closest people.

TESTATOR AND 2 WITNESSES WHILE TOGETHER SIGN WILL
This Will after being filled out (except bits intentionally left blank) must be signed by the person doing the Will (the "Testator") in front of at least 2 persons acting as witnesses at least age 18 who then also sign.

LAST WILL AND TESTAMENT

I, _____, of _____, North Carolina, do revoke all prior Wills and testamentary documents and do make, publish, and declare this as my Will. I am of sound mind and under no duress or undue influence and act voluntarily.

1. LIVING SPOUSE AND CHILDREN. To show I am mentally fit and have sufficient memory to do a Will I do say I now have the following living spouse and living children: _____
_____.

2. GIFTS. I give these gifts in this Will, but to get a gift in this section the recipient must survive me except as otherwise stated below.

I give _____ to _____.
I give _____ to _____.
I give _____ to _____.
I give _____ to _____.
I give _____ to _____.
I give _____ to _____.
I give _____ to _____.
I give _____ to _____.
I give _____ to _____.
I give _____ to _____.
I give _____ to _____.

3. RESIDUE. The rest, residue, and remainder of my estate, and anything else, I give:
 a) to _____ who survive me, and with persons just named who survive me taking the share of non-survivors, then if anything remains
 b) to _____ and if any of those just now named do not survive me their part goes to their lineal descendants per stirpes.

4. ADMINISTRATION. I name, nominate, and appoint _____ as Personal Representative including for me, my Will, and my estate.

5. GUARDIAN. I name _____ to be Guardian Of The Person of any minor child of mine and to have care, authority, custody, and other control of them. I name this same person to be Guardian Of The Estate for any minor child and to have care, control, and power over their property, money, and estate

6. MISCELLANEOUS. The following applies to this Will and generally.

In this Will no part left unfilled is a mistake including spaces in the residue clause.

The facts support and I want North Carolina law to apply to this Will and my estate.

I order that my just debts, funeral and related expenses, and taxes be paid as soon after my death as practical but only those items my Personal Representative chooses to pay.

Priority of Will gifts of the same type is based on the order they are made in this Will.

The words give and gift also means a devise, bequest, grant, legacy, or similar.

I am intentionally not providing by Will or other ways for some family, including I am not providing for some children of mine and also children of a deceased child of mine.

If a Will gift reasonably mentions survival then survival is an absolute condition and anti-lapse laws or similar provisions have no effect and without survival the gift lapses. Unless a Will gift specifies otherwise if a Will gift goes to multiple recipients if any do not survive me the part to them lapses and instead goes to other surviving recipients.

No earlier transfer reduces a Will gift unless I usually called it a loan or advancement.

In this Will any gendered word includes all genders, and the singular includes the plural and vice versa, and they can mean a single person or many persons.

Unless a Will specifically says otherwise a secured debt including a mortgage or lien shall not be paid off including by a Personal Representative or in probate, and a recipient of a Will gift of property takes it subject to debts. Also, no recipient of property who may lose it or who pays to keep it may have my estate or others pay or do exoneration.

If I somehow lost ownership of an item in a specific Will gift the gift is extinguished.

I request and authorize any informal, summary, and quick probate or similar action. Any Personal Representative may act independently with no supervision of any court, including independent administration, and with no inventory, appraisal, or other action.

I give any Personal Representative the a) fullest authority, discretion, and powers allowed by state law, b) power to lease, sell, mortgage, convey, or keep property including real property in a manner and time they deem helpful or proper, and c) authority to settle or pay claims or debts in the time and manner they choose. Any Personal Representative or other fiduciary shall have all powers and authorities that may be given by statute or common law in any jurisdiction they may act, including under North Carolina law.

Any Guardian of any type, Conservator, Custodian, or other person managing a minor's property or money may use or invade the principal and sell property without court action.

If context permits the terms Personal Representative and Executor and Administrator are interchangeable, Conservator and Guardian of the Estate and Guardian of Property and Custodian are interchangeable, and residue and residuary are interchangeable. Any such

person may stand in the place of and have all powers like the others named here.

The residue includes lapsed or failed gifts, insurance paid to the estate, digital assets, inheritances owed me, and all I had power of appointment or testamentary disposition over.

Any Personal Representative may access, manage, delete, modify, transfer, and otherwise control any digital accounts and assets I had any interest in or power over.

Any Personal Representative, Executor, Administrator, Guardian of any type like for a person or estate, Conservator, Custodian, and any other fiduciary under this Will or otherwise shall qualify and serve without bond, surety, security, surety bond, or similar.

If evidence does not show it likely a person survived me by 120 hours (5 days) then for this Will and my estate they shall be deemed in all ways as having died before me.

If part of this Will is by law invalid or unenforceable other provisions remain in effect.

Any Personal Representative may at any time transfer money or property of a minor under age 18 to a Custodian to act under the North Carolina Uniform Transfers to Minors Act or similar law anywhere, and may pick a person to be Custodian including themselves.

TESTATOR

IN WITNESS WHEREOF, I, _____, the Testator, sign my name to this instrument this, and do hereby declare that I sign and execute this instrument as my Will and that I sign it willingly, that I execute it as my free and voluntary act for the purposes therein expressed, and that I am 18 years of age or older, of sound mind, and under no constraint or undue influence.

_____
Signature of Testator

WITNESSES

We, _____ and _____, the Witnesses, sign our names to this instrument, and do hereby declare that the Testator signs and executes this instrument as the Will of the Testator in our presence and that the Testator signs it willingly, and that each of us at the request of the Testator and in the presence and hearing of the Testator, and in the presence and hearing of each other, hereby signs this Will to function legally as witness to the Testator's signing, and to the best of our knowledge the Testator is eighteen years of age or older, of sound mind, and under no constraint or undue influence.

_____ _____
Signature of Witness #1   Address of Witness #1

_____ _____
Signature of Witness #2   Address of Witness #2

CHAPTER 9
FORM 3: SELF-PROVING AFFIDAVIT

FORM CAN BE DONE TO HELP WITH THE WORK OF USING A WILL LATER

This form is optional but can be done right after a Will is done, or anytime afterward, to help with the legal work that is involved in later using a Will after a death. This form is a statutory form that is found in North Carolina law at N.C. General Statutes § 31-11.6

FORM HELPS SHOW A WILL WAS PROPERLY SIGNED

The Self-Proving Affidavit helps "prove" a Will was signed properly. If this form isn't done then after a death a little more work is needed to get evidence from either witnesses to the Will signing, persons familiar with signatures of people, or a handwriting expert. Without the Self-Proving Affidavit there is a bit more legal risk a Will won't be followed later. But of people doing Wills about half skip a Self-Proving Affidavit mostly due to the hassle of finding a notary on top of 2 witnesses each time a Will is done, and since it requires extra work by the person doing a Will mostly just to save later work of people happy to be getting things under a Will.

FORM IS DONE BY TESTATOR AND 2 WITNESSES SIGNING WITH A NOTARY

For this form to be valid a person who is a notary (also called a "notary public") must see the Testator and 2 witnesses sign this form and then the notary notarizes the form. A notary can be found and asked to help at a bank, insurance agent, government office, or by first using a phonebook. This form is often done a few minutes after a Will is signed but it also can be done later (even years later) when everyone can meet with a notary. But this form can't be done before a Will is done. This form when it is completed is often kept paper-clipped to the Will it supports.

SELF-PROVING AFFIDAVIT

(North Carolina General Statutes § 31-11.6)

STATE OF NORTH CAROLINA
COUNTY / CITY OF _____

Before me, the undersigned authority, on this day personally appeared _____, _____, and _____, known to me to be the Testator and the Witnesses, respectively, whose names are signed to the attached or foregoing instrument and, all of these persons being by me first duly sworn. The Testator, declared to me and to the Witnesses in my presence: That said instrument is the Will of the Testator; that the Testator had willingly signed, and executed it in the presence of said Witnesses as the Testator's free and voluntary act for the purposes therein expressed; or, that the testator signified that the instrument was his instrument by acknowledging to them his signature previously affixed thereto.

The said Witnesses stated before me that the foregoing Will was acknowledged and executed by the Testator as the Will of the Testator in the presence of said Witnesses who, in the presence of the Testator and at the request of Testator, subscribed their names thereto to function as attesting witnesses and that the Testator, at the time of the execution of said will, was over the age of 18 years and of sound and disposing mind and memory.

_____
Testator

_____   _____
Witness   Witness

Subscribed, sworn and acknowledged before me by _____, the testator, subscribed and sworn before me by _____ and _____, witnesses, this _____ day of _____, 20____.

(SEAL)   Signature of Notary or Officer: _____

CHAPTER 10
FORM 4: HANDWRITTEN WILL

WILL CAN SKIP USING THE NORMAL 2 WITNESSES IF IT'S HANDWRITTEN
A Handwritten Will is a Will that is easier to do since it does not need the usual 2 witnesses to a Will.

HANDWRITTEN WILL WITHOUT WITNESSES IS ALLOWED IN MAINE
In 27 states including North Carolina a person doing a Will can skip using the usual 2 Will witnesses if: 1) it is all handwritten by the person doing the Will (not photocopied, typed, computer printed, or handwritten by anyone else), and 2) it is signed and dated. Many people call this a Handwritten Will but most lawyers call it a Holographic Will (holo means whole and graph means image in the Greek language). These Wills are allowed since handwriting is harder to fake, people may be in an emergency or rush, witnesses may be scarce in the countryside, it is private, it can be cheap by skipping complexity and people, and it is traditional to allow this especially in rural places. North Carolina law use to require a Handwritten Will be kept with other important papers but since 2021 this is no longer required at all. The 27 states with Handwritten Wills have 55% of the U.S. population. See states with Handwritten Wills on map below in dark.

■ 27 STATES ALLOW HANDWRITTEN WILL WITHOUT 2 WITNESSES

HANDWRITTEN WILLS ARE USUALLY FINE BUT REQUIRE LATER WORK
Some lawyers warn against Handwritten Wills saying they often read confusingly, skip legal words that help in some cases, and are found invalid more often – but some studies show they are liked and usually fine. To use a Handwritten Will later after a death some people must in writing or in testimony say the handwriting looks like the Testator's, which can be a hassle. But a normal Will if no Self-Proving Affidavit was done also needs similar proof like from a witness to the signing or other proof of signing. Handwritten Wills tend to be done by people who are young so unlikely to need a Will soon, who are in a hurry, who want to fix a mistake, who before a trip want to pick a Guardian, who moved to a new state, or who plan to do a better Will later.

WORDS BELOW ON THIS PAGE CAN BE USED FOR A HANDWRITTEN WILL

People can do a Handwritten Will in a sentence that is legal but may leave out helpful parts, for example: *"As my Will I give my estate and all else to Ann Baker who shall be Executor. - Dan Baker"* But it is recommended people use more complex words for a Handwritten Will shown on this page below. To do this people should change the names and words below on this page to match what they want done. If some people named to get things later die it is best to quickly re-do the Will and name different people. The last paragraph about Guardians for children can be skipped if a person has no children under age 18. This Will must be all handwritten by the person doing it on some paper (pencil is allowed) and then signed and dated by the person (usually in pen or permanent marker).

WILL

1. I am John Max Hill and I now live in Wake County, North Carolina. I revoke any prior Wills and Codicils and declare this to be my Will.

2. I give my property, money, estate, and all else to Jane Eve Hill and Ann Lee Baker. My not giving to other family members is intentional.

3. I name Jane Eve Hill as Personal Representative for me, my Will, and my estate. I request informal probate.

4. No bond or surety is needed for any Personal Representative or any Guardian of any type.

5. If ever needed for a minor child I name Mary Ann Dodd as Guardian of the Person to have care, custody, and control of them.
I name this same person as Guardian of the Estate to have control and power over any minor child's property, money, and estate.

May 8, 2024   *John Max Hill*

CHAPTER 11
FORM 5: HEALTH CARE POWER OF ATTORNEY

FORM CAN NAME HEALTH CARE AGENT AND GIVE INSTRUCTIONS

This form lets a person if they want name someone as Agent to make health care decisions if person is later incapacitated, and if wanted write health care instructions. Many people do this 1 health care form and skip other health care forms. But paramedics and similar people usually will usually not follow this form. This is a statutory form found at N. C. General Statutes § 32A-25.1 and it can be found online many places like the Secretary State's office at https://www.sosnc.gov/forms/by_title/_advance_healthcare_directives.

IN FORM CAN NAME AGENT TO HAVE POWER OVER HEALTH CARE

This form lets a person name someone as "Agent" to make medical decisions if person is incapacitated (usually this means by inability to be conscious, be rational, or communicate). Often named as Agent is a spouse, relative, or friend. Naming a person as Agent can avoid them having to rush to see a judge later. An Agent should do what person would probably want, obey written instructions, obey verbal instructions clearly said to them, but in general can use some judgment. Many people skip naming a 2nd person to serve as Agent is needed (a "successor") since usually the 1st person named will be available.

IN FORM GIVE HEALTH CARE INSTRUCTIONS

In the form a person can give written health care instructions that family, Agent, and doctors must follow. But many people skip written instructions since they are hard to write to cover all medical situations, they can cause delay and lawsuits if not clear, and many people trust an Agent's or family's wisdom to do what's best. People can name an Agent but skip instructions, or do instructions and skip an Agent. The form has options about withholding care near end-of-life but many people skip this and trust an Agent or family, or they do a separate 'Living Will" (this book has this form). Many people skip options on a funeral and organ donation. Some places ask people write 1 or 2 sentences of "limitations", and this should be done above the words: **"NOTE: DO NOT initial unless you insert a limitation."**

MUST SIGN FORM USING WITNESSES AND A NOTARY

To do the form a person signs while present with 2 witnesses and a person who is notary, and then the witnesses sign, and then the notary signs and notarizes the form. Witnesses must be at least 18 and can't
  a) be a relative or their spouse (not a child, parent, aunt/uncle, cousin, grandparent, or grandchild),
  b) be likely to inherit by Will or benefit financially other ways (so not a friend named in a Will),
  c) be the attending physician or a paid employee of any health care facility being used, or
  d) have debt or other claims against the person or their estate.

Once completed usually people show the form to places they are getting treatment at. Many people keep a copy by a bedside table, fridge, or their body. The North Carolina Secretary of State has set up an optional "Advanced Health Care Directive Registry" at **www.sosnc.gov/ahcdr** to let people file a form and just keep a card near them so it is seen, but this is optional and fairly uncommon. Most people tell family their plans. To revoke this form a person usually tells any person given power, family, and places that saw the form.

STATE OF NORTH CAROLINA

COUNTY OF _____

HEALTH CARE POWER OF ATTORNEY

NOTE: YOU SHOULD USE THIS DOCUMENT TO NAME A PERSON AS YOUR HEALTH CARE AGENT IF YOU ARE COMFORTABLE GIVING THAT PERSON BROAD AND SWEEPING POWERS TO MAKE HEALTH CARE DECISIONS FOR YOU. THERE IS NO LEGAL REQUIREMENT THAT ANYONE EXECUTE A HEALTH CARE POWER OF ATTORNEY.

> *EXPLANATION:* You have the right to name someone to make health care decisions for you when you cannot make or communicate those decisions. This form may be used to create a health care power of attorney, and meets the requirements of North Carolina law. However, you are not required to use this form, and North Carolina law allows the use of other forms that meet certain requirements. If you prepare your own health care power of attorney, you should be very careful to make sure it is consistent with North Carolina law.
>
> This document gives the person you designate as your health care agent **broad powers** to make health care decisions for you when you cannot make the decision yourself or cannot communicate your decision to other people. You should discuss your wishes concerning life-prolonging measures, mental health treatment, and other health care decisions with your health care agent. Except to the extent that you express specific limitations or restrictions in this form, your health care agent may make any health care decision you could make yourself.
>
> This form does not impose a duty on your health care agent to exercise granted powers, but when a power is exercised, your health care agent will be obligated to use due care to act in your best interests and in accordance with this document.
>
> This Health Care Power of Attorney form is intended to be valid in any jurisdiction in which it is presented, but places outside North Carolina may impose requirements that this form does not meet.
>
> If you want to use this form, you must complete it, sign it, and have your signature witnessed by two qualified witnesses and proved by a notary public. Follow the instructions about which choices you can initial very carefully. **Do not sign this form until** two witnesses and a notary public are present to watch you sign it. You then should give a copy to your health care agent and to any alternates you name. You should consider filing it with the Advance Health Care Directive Registry maintained by the North Carolina Secretary of State: http://www.sosnc.gov/health.

1. **Designation of Health Care Agent.**

I, _____, being of sound mind, **hereby appoint the following person(s) to serve as my health care agent(s)** to act for me and in my name (in any way I could act in person) to make health care decisions for me as authorized in this document. **My designated health care agent(s) shall serve alone, in the order named.**

A. Name: _____   Home Telephone: _____
Home Address: _____   Work Telephone: _____
_____   Cellular Telephone: _____

B. Name: _____   Home Telephone: _____
Home Address: _____   Work Telephone: _____
_____   Cellular Telephone: _____

C. Name: _____   Home Telephone: _____
Home Address: _____   Work Telephone: _____
_____   Cellular Telephone: _____

Any successor health care agent designated shall be vested with the same power and duties as if originally named as my health care agent, and shall serve any time his or her predecessor is not reasonably available or is unwilling or unable to serve in that capacity.

2. Effectiveness of Appointment.

My designation of a health care agent expires only when I revoke it. Absent revocation, the authority granted in this document shall become effective when and if one of the physician(s) listed below determines that I lack capacity to make or communicate decisions relating to my health care, and will continue in effect during that incapacity, or until my death, except if I authorize my health care agent to exercise my rights with respect to anatomical gifts, autopsy, or disposition of my remains, this authority will continue after my death to the extent necessary to exercise that authority.

1. _____ *(Physician)*   2. _____ *(Physician)*

If I have not designated a physician, or no physician(s) named above is reasonably available, the determination that I lack capacity to make or communicate decisions relating to my health care shall be made by my attending physician.

3. Revocation.

Any time while I am competent, I may revoke this power of attorney in a writing I sign or by communicating my intent to revoke, in any clear and consistent manner, to my health care agent or my health care provider.

4. General Statement of Authority Granted.

Subject to any restrictions set forth in Section 5 below, I grant to my health care agent full power and authority to make and carry out all health care decisions for me. These decisions include, but are not limited to:

 A. Requesting, reviewing, and receiving any information, verbal or written, regarding my physical or mental health, including, but not limited to, medical and hospital records, and to consent to the disclosure of this information.

 B. Employing or discharging my health care providers.

 C. Consenting to and authorizing my admission to and discharge from a hospital, nursing or convalescent home, hospice, long-term care facility, or other health care facility.

 D. Consenting to and authorizing my admission to and retention in a facility for care or treatment of mental illness.

 E. Consenting to and authorizing the administration of medications for mental health treatment and electroconvulsive treatment (ECT) commonly referred to as "shock treatment."

F. Giving consent for, withdrawing consent for, or withholding consent for, X-ray, anesthesia, medication, surgery, and all other diagnostic and treatment procedures ordered by or under the authorization of a licensed physician, dentist, podiatrist, or other health care provider. This authorization specifically includes the power to consent to measures for relief of pain.

G. Authorizing the withholding or withdrawal of life-prolonging measures.

H. Providing my medical information at the request of any individual acting as my attorney-in-fact under a durable power of attorney or as a Trustee or successor Trustee under any Trust Agreement of which I am a Grantor or Trustee, or at the request of any other individual whom my health care agent believes should have such information. I desire that such information be provided whenever it would expedite the prompt and proper handling of my affairs or the affairs of any person or entity for which I have some responsibility. In addition, I authorize my health care agent to take any and all legal steps necessary to ensure compliance with my instructions providing access to my protected health information. Such steps shall include resorting to any and all legal procedures in and out of courts as may be necessary to enforce my rights under the law and shall include attempting to recover attorneys' fees against anyone who does not comply with this health care power of attorney.

I. To the extent I have not already made valid and enforceable arrangements during my lifetime that have not been revoked, exercising any right I may have to authorize an autopsy or direct the disposition of my remains.

J. Taking any lawful actions that may be necessary to carry out these decisions, including, but not limited to: (i) signing, executing, delivering, and acknowledging any agreement, release, authorization, or other document that may be necessary, desirable, convenient, or proper in order to exercise and carry out any of these powers; (ii) granting releases of liability to medical providers or others; and (iii) incurring reasonable costs on my behalf related to exercising these powers, provided that this health care power of attorney shall not give my health care agent general authority over my property or financial affairs.

5. Special Provisions and Limitations.

(Notice: The authority granted in this document is intended to be as broad as possible so that your health care agent will have authority to make any decisions you could make to obtain or terminate any type of health care treatment or service. If you wish to limit the scope of your health care agent's powers, you may do so in this section. If none of the following are initialed, there will be no special limitations to your agent's authority.)

	A. <u>Limitations about Artificial Nutrition or Hydration</u>: In exercising the authority to make health care decisions on my behalf, my health care agent:
_____ (Initial)	Shall NOT have the authority to withhold artificial nutrition (such as through tubes) OR may exercise that authority only in accordance with the following special provisions:
_____ (Initial)	Shall NOT have the authority to withhold artificial hydration (such as through tubes) OR may exercise that authority only in accordance with the following special provisions:
	NOTE: If you initial either block but do not insert any special provisions, your health care agent shall have NO AUTHORITY to withhold artificial nutrition or hydration.

(Initial)	B. <u>Limitations Concerning Health Care Decisions.</u> In exercising the authority to make health care decisions on my behalf, the authority of my health care agent is subject to the following special provisions: (Here you may include any specific provisions you deem appropriate such as: your own definition of when life-prolonging measures should be withheld or discontinued, or instructions to refuse any specific types of treatment that are inconsistent with your religious beliefs, or are unacceptable to you for any other reason.)
	NOTE: DO NOT initial unless you insert a limitation.
(Initial)	C. <u>Limitations Concerning Mental Health Decisions.</u> In exercising the authority to make mental health decisions on my behalf, the authority of my health care agent is subject to following special provisions: (Here you may include any specific provisions you deem appropriate such as: limiting the grant of authority to make only mental health treatment decisions, your own instructions regarding the administration or withholding of psychotropic medications and electroconvulsive treatment (ECT), instructions regarding your admission to and retention in a health care facility for mental health treatment, or instructions to refuse any specific types of treatment that are unacceptable to you.)
	NOTE: DO NOT initial unless you insert a limitation.
(Initial)	D. <u>Advance Instruction for Mental Health Treatment.</u> (Notice: This health care power of attorney may incorporate or be combined with an advance instruction for mental health treatment, executed in accordance with Part 2 of Article 3 of Chapter 122C of the General Statutes, which you may use to state your instructions regarding mental health treatment in the event you lack capacity to make or communicate mental health treatment decisions. Because your health care agent's decisions must be consistent with any statements you have expressed in an advance instruction, you should indicate here whether you have executed an advance instruction for mental health treatment):
	NOTE: DO NOT initial unless you insert a limitation.
(Initial)	E. <u>Autopsy and Disposition of Remains.</u> In exercising the authority to make decisions regarding autopsy and disposition of remains on my behalf, the authority of my health care agent is subject to the following special provisions and limitations. (Here you may include any specific limitations you deem appropriate such as: limiting the grant of authority and the scope of authority, or instructions regarding burial or cremation):
	NOTE: DO NOT initial unless you insert a limitation.

6. Organ Donation.

To the extent I have not already made valid and enforceable arrangements during my lifetime that have not been revoked, my health care agent may exercise any right I may have to:

(Initial)	donate any needed organs or parts; or
(Initial)	donate only the following organs or parts: _____
	NOTE: DO NOT INITIAL BOTH BLOCKS ABOVE.
(Initial)	donate my body for anatomical study if needed.
(Initial)	In exercising the authority to make donations, my health care agent is subject to the following special provisions and limitations: (Here you may include any specific limitations you deem appropriate such as: limiting the grant of authority and the scope of authority, or instructions regarding gifts of the body or body parts.) _____
	NOTE: DO NOT initial unless you insert a limitation.

NOTE: NO AUTHORITY FOR ORGAN DONATION IS GRANTED IN THIS INSTRUMENT WITHOUT YOUR INITIALS.

7. Guardianship Provision.

If it becomes necessary for a court to appoint a guardian of my person, I nominate the persons designated in Section 1, in the order named, to be the guardian of my person, to serve without bond or security. The guardian shall act consistently with G.S. 35A-1201(a)(5).

8. Reliance of Third Parties on Health Care Agent.

A. No person who relies in good faith upon the authority of or any representations by my health care agent shall be liable to me, my estate, my heirs, successors, assigns, or personal representatives, for actions or omissions in reliance on that authority or those representations.

B. The powers conferred on my health care agent by this document may be exercised by my health care agent alone, and my health care agent's signature or action taken under the authority granted in this document may be accepted by persons as fully authorized by me and with the same force and effect as if I were personally present, competent, and acting on my own behalf. All acts performed in good faith by my health care agent pursuant to this power of attorney are done with my consent and shall have the same validity and effect as if I were present and exercised the powers myself, and shall inure to the benefit of and bind me, my estate, my heirs, successors, assigns, and personal representatives. The authority of my health care agent pursuant to this power of attorney shall be superior to and binding upon my family, relatives, friends, and others.

9. **Miscellaneous Provisions.**

    A. Revocation of Prior Powers of Attorney. I revoke any prior health care power of attorney. The preceding sentence is not intended to revoke any general powers of attorney, some of the provisions of which may relate to health care; however, this power of attorney shall take precedence over any health care provisions in any valid general power of attorney I have not revoked.

    B. Jurisdiction, Severability, and Durability. This Health Care Power of Attorney is intended to be valid in any jurisdiction in which it is presented. The powers delegated under this power of attorney are severable, so that the invalidity of one or more powers shall not affect any others. This power of attorney shall not be affected or revoked by my incapacity or mental incompetence.

    C. Health Care Agent Not Liable. My health care agent and my health care agent's estate, heirs, successors, and assigns are hereby released and forever discharged by me, my estate, my heirs, successors, assigns, and personal representatives from all liability and from all claims or demands of all kinds arising out of my health care agent's acts or omissions, except for my health care agent's willful misconduct or gross negligence.

    D. No Civil or Criminal Liability. No act or omission of my health care agent, or of any other person, entity, institution, or facility acting in good faith in reliance on the authority of my health care agent pursuant to this Health Care Power of Attorney shall be considered suicide, nor the cause of my death for any civil or criminal purposes, nor shall it be considered unprofessional conduct or as lack of professional competence. Any person, entity, institution, or facility against whom criminal or civil liability is asserted because of conduct authorized by this Health Care Power of Attorney may interpose this document as a defense.

    E. Reimbursement. My health care agent shall be entitled to reimbursement for all reasonable expenses incurred as a result of carrying out any provision of this directive.

SIGNATURE: By signing here, I indicate that I am mentally alert and competent, fully informed as to the contents of this document, and understand the full import of this grant of powers to my health care agent.

This the _____ day of _____, 20____.

_____ (SEAL)

WITNESSES: I hereby state that the principal, _____, being of sound mind, signed (or directed another to sign on the principal's behalf) the foregoing health care power of attorney in my presence, and that I am not related to the principal by blood or marriage, and I would not be entitled to any portion of the estate of the principal under any existing will or codicil of the principal or as an heir under the Intestate Succession Act, if the principal died on this date without a will. I also state that I am not the principal's attending physician, nor a licensed health care provider or mental health treatment provider who is (1) an employee of the principal's attending physician or mental health treatment provider, (2) an employee of the health facility in which the principal is a patient, or (3) an employee of a nursing home or any adult care home where the principal resides. I further state that I do not have any claim against the principal or estate of the principal.

Date: _____ Witness: _____

Date: _____ Witness: _____

NOTARY:

_____ **COUNTY, NORTH CAROLINA STATE**

Sworn to (or affirmed) and subscribed before me this day by _____
                                                              (type/print name of signer)

_____   _____
(type/print name of witness)   *(type/print name of witness)*

Date: _____   Signature of Notary Public: _____
                                  Printed or typed name of Notary Public: _____
(Official Seal)   My commission expires: _____

CHAPTER 12
FORM 6: ADVANCE DIRECTIVE FOR A NATURAL DEATH ("LIVING WILL")

IN FORM CAN SAY WHEN TO LATER STOP HEALTH CARE

This form lets a person do the serious act of saying stop most health care if <u>later</u> they're incapacitated and doctors think the person's health is very bad and <u>more health care likely won't help</u>. But when not inside some facility the paramedics and others usually will <u>not</u> follow this complicated form. This is a statutory form found at N. C. General Statutes § 90-321 and it can be found online many places like the Secretary State's office at *https://www.sosnc.gov/forms/by_title/_advance_healthcare_directives*. This form is rarely used.

IN FORM CAN PICK HOW BAD MUST HEALTH BE BEFORE TREATMENT STOPS

This form lets a person do the serious act of saying stop most health care if <u>later</u> doctors think the person's health is very bad and more health care likely won't help. This form only matters if a person is incapacitated so can't tell doctors what to do, like by inability to be conscious, be rational, or communicate. In the form a person must initial several places to pick options. No matter what pain relief and comfort care is usually always given. A person not incapacitated is free to later undo the form, like by telling a doctor or nurse, "I changed my mind and from now on want to get all medical care, and want to cancel my Living Will." <u>Most people skip this form</u> since rarely are people incapacitated and then live that long, limiting care can risk causing some problems or mistakes, since these issues are stressful, and since many people trust their family and others to make wise decisions if needed.

MUST SIGN FORM USING WITNESSES AND A NOTARY

To do the form <u>a person signs while present with 2 witnesses and a person who is notary, and then the witnesses sign, and then the notary signs and notarizes the form</u>. Witnesses must be at least 18 and <u>can't</u>
   a) be a relative or their spouse (not a child, parent, aunt/uncle, cousin, grandparent, or grandchild),
   b) be likely to inherit by Will or benefit financially other ways (so not a friend named in a Will),
   c) be the attending physician or a paid employee of any health care facility being used, or
   d) have debt or other claims against the person or their estate.
Once completed usually people show the form to places they are getting treatment at. The North Carolina Secretary of State has set up an optional "Advanced Health Care Directive Registry" for people to use at **www.sosnc.gov/ahcdr** to let people file a form and just keep a card near them <u>so it is seen</u>, but this is optional and fairly uncommon. Most people tell family their plans. To revoke this form a person usually tells any person given power, family, and places that saw the form.

STATE OF NORTH CAROLINA

COUNTY OF _____

ADVANCE DIRECTIVE FOR A NATURAL DEATH ("LIVING WILL")

NOTE: YOU SHOULD USE THIS DOCUMENT TO GIVE YOUR HEALTH CARE PROVIDERS INSTRUCTIONS TO WITHHOLD OR WITHDRAW LIFE PROLONGING MEASURES IN CERTAIN SITUATIONS. THERE IS NO LEGAL REQUIREMENT THAT ANYONE EXECUTE A LIVING WILL.

GENERAL INSTRUCTIONS: You can use this Advance Directive ("Living Will") form to give instructions for the future if you want your health care providers to withhold or withdraw life-prolonging measures in certain situations. You should talk to your doctor about what these terms mean. The Living Will states what choices you would have made for yourself if you were able to communicate. Talk to your family members, friends, and others you trust about your choices. Also, it is a good idea to talk with professionals such as your doctors, clergypersons, and lawyers before you complete and sign this Living Will.

You do not have to use this form to give those instructions, but if you create your own Advance Directive you need to be very careful to ensure that it is consistent with North Carolina law.

This Living Will form is intended to be valid in any jurisdiction in which it is presented, but places outside North Carolina may impose requirements that this form does not meet.

If you want to use this form, you must complete it, sign it, and have your signature witnessed by two qualified witnesses and proved by a notary public. Follow the instructions about which choices you can initial very carefully. **Do not sign this form until two witnesses and a notary public are present to watch you sign it.** *You then should consider giving a copy to your primary physician and/or a trusted relative, and should consider filing it with the Advanced Health Care Directive Registry maintained by the North Carolina Secretary of State: http://www.sosnc.gov/health.*

MY DESIRE FOR A NATURAL DEATH

I, _____, being of sound mind, desire that, as specified below, my life not be prolonged by life-prolonging measures:

1. When My Directives Apply

My directions about prolonging my life shall apply *IF* my attending physician determines that I lack capacity to make or communicate health care decisions and:

NOTE: YOU MAY INITIAL ANY OR ALL OF THESE CHOICES.

(Initial)	I have an incurable or irreversible condition that will result in my death within a relatively short period of time.
(Initial)	I become unconscious and my health care providers determine that, to a high degree of medical certainty, I will never regain my consciousness.
(Initial)	I suffer from advanced dementia or any other condition which results in the substantial loss of my cognitive ability and my health care providers determine that, to a high degree of medical certainty, this loss is not reversible.

2. These are My Directives about Prolonging My Life:

In those situations I have initialed in Section 1, I direct that my health care providers:

NOTE: INITIAL ONLY IN ONE PLACE.

(Initial)	may withhold or withdraw life-prolonging measures.
(Initial)	shall withhold or withdraw life-prolonging measures.

3. Exceptions – "Artificial Nutrition or Hydration"

NOTE: INITIAL ONLY IF YOU WANT TO MAKE EXCEPTIONS TO YOUR INSTRUCTIONS IN PARAGRAPH 2.

EVEN THOUGH I do not want my life prolonged in those situations I have initialed in Section 1:

(Initial)	I *DO* want to receive BOTH artificial hydration AND artificial nutrition (for example, through tubes) in those situations.
	NOTE: DO NOT INITIAL THIS BLOCK IF ONE OF THE BLOCKS BELOW IS INITIALED.
(Initial)	I *DO* want to receive ONLY artificial hydration (for example, by tubes) in those situations.
	NOTE: DO NOT INITIAL THE BLOCK ABOVE OR BELOW IF THIS BLOCK IS INITIALED.
(Initial)	I *DO* want to receive ONLY artificial nutrition (for example, through tubes) in those situations.
	NOTE: DO NOT INITIAL EITHER OF THE TWO BLOCKS ABOVE IF THIS BLOCK IS INITIALED.

4. I Wish to be Made as Comfortable as Possible

I direct that my health care providers take reasonable steps to keep me as clean, comfortable, and free of pain as possible so that my dignity is maintained, even though this care may hasten my death.

5. I Understand my Advance Directive

I am aware and understand that this document directs certain life-prolonging measures to be withheld or discontinued in accordance with my advance instructions.

6. If I have an Available Health Care Agent

If I have appointed a health care agent by executing a health care power of attorney or similar instrument, and that health care agent is acting and available and gives instructions that differ from this Advance Directive, then I direct that:

(Initial)	<u>Follow Advance Directive:</u> This Advance Directive will override instructions my health care agent gives about prolonging my life.
(Initial)	<u>Follow Health Care Agent:</u> My health care agent has authority to **override** this Advance Directive.

NOTE: **DO NOT INITIAL BOTH BLOCKS.** *IF YOU DO NOT INITIAL EITHER BOX, THEN YOUR HEALTH CARE PROVIDERS WILL FOLLOW THIS ADVANCE DIRECTIVE AND IGNORE THE INSTRUCTIONS OF YOUR HEALTH CARE AGENT ABOUT PROLONGING YOUR LIFE.*

7. My Health Care Providers May Rely on this Directive

My health care providers shall not be liable to me or to my family, my estate, my heirs, or my personal representative for following the instructions I give in this instrument. Following my directions shall not be considered suicide, or the cause of my death, or malpractice or unprofessional conduct. If I have revoked this instrument but my health care providers do not know that I have done so, and they follow the instructions in this instrument in good faith, they shall be entitled to the same protections to which they would have been entitled if the instrument had not been revoked.

8.   I Want this Directive to be Effective Anywhere

I intend that this Advance Directive be followed by any health care provider in any place.

9.   I have the Right to Revoke this Advance Directive

I understand that at any time I may revoke this Advance Directive in a writing I sign or by communicating in any clear and consistent manner my intent to revoke it to my attending physician. I understand that if I revoke this instrument I should try to destroy all copies of it.

SIGNATURE:

This the _____ day of _____, 20_____.

_____
Signature of Declarant

_____
Type/Print Name

WITNESSES:

I hereby state that the declarant, _____, being of sound mind, signed (or directed another to sign on declarant's behalf) the foregoing Advance Directive for a Natural Death in my presence, and that I am not related to the declarant by blood or marriage, and I would not be entitled to any portion of the estate of the declarant under any existing will or codicil of the declarant or as an heir under the Intestate Succession Act, if the declarant died on this date without a will. I also state that I am not the declarant's attending physician, nor a licensed health care provider who is (1) an employee of the declarant's attending physician, (2) nor an employee of the health facility in which the declarant is a patient, or (3) an employee of a nursing home or any adult care home where the declarant resides. I further state that I do not have any claim against the declarant or the estate of the declarant.

Date: _____   Witness: _____

Date: _____   Witness: _____

NOTARY:

_____COUNTY, NORTH CAROLINA STATE

Sworn to (or affirmed) and subscribed before me this day by _____
                                                                (type/print name of declarant)

_____   _____
(type/print name of witness)   *(type/print name of witness)*

Date: _____   *Signature of Notary Public:*_____
                                                         *Printed or typed name of Notary Public:*_____
     (Official Seal)   My commission expires: _____

CHAPTER 13
FORM 7: DO NOT RESUSCITATE

IN FORM CAN IMMEDIATELY REFUSE MOST HEALTH CARE

This chapter actually has 2 forms which are similar and people pick from to do the serious act of saying to immediately no longer give most or certain health care. Doing this is serious and often only the sickest or oldest people do it. Both forms are often called the "Do Not Resuscitate" or "DNR" form and will usually be followed by paramedics and other personnel not in a facility, but other forms often won't be followed by them. These 2 forms are available many places including from the paramedics agency, the Office Of Emergency Medical Services, at https://oems.nc.gov/dnr-most. Usually a person only does 1 of these 2 forms.

FIRST FORM SAYS TO IMMEDIATELY NOT GIVE MANY KINDS OF CARE

This chapter's first form, the "Medical Orders For Life-Sustaining Treatment" form (the "M.O.S.T." form), says to immediately not give the many kinds of health care named in it. This form can say to immediately no longer try C.P.R., antibiotics, and artificial feeding. This form is short so it can be read fast and be followed by those in a hurry like paramedics outside any care facility, but this form is more often used by people who are in a care facility. Pain relief and comfort care is usually still given, so paramedics are still usually called if needed to get this. After doing this form a person is usually free to override it by clearly requesting care from a doctor, paramedic, or other person. In recent years the M.O.S.T. form is the form most often used to say to immediately not give care, and other forms are less often used including this chapter's second form.

SECOND FORM SAYS TO IMMEDIATELY NOT TRY RESUSCITATION

This chapter's second form, the "Do Not Resuscitate" form (often called the "D-N-R" form or similar) says to immediately not give any resuscitation. Resuscitation is trying to restart or help with breathing or the heart and usually covers cardio-pulmonary resuscitation (C.P.R.), defibrillation (electric shocks), and machine or tube breathing. This form is short so it can be read fast and followed by those in a hurry like paramedics, and this form is more often used by people outside and not in a care facility. Pain relief and comfort care is usually still given, so paramedics are still usually called if needed to get this. After doing this form a person is usually free to override it by clearly requesting care from a doctor, paramedic, or other person.

FORM IS SIGNED BY DOCTOR OR SIMILAR AND THEN THE PATIENT

To be valid form these forms must be signed by a person's doctor (physician) or other similar health professional, and usually by the person doing it (or their named representative if authorized to do this). Once done people usually people show a form to places that may give care to add it medical files to follow. Often people keep a copy of the form near their body to show to paramedics or others who try to give care. Some people with a Do Not Resuscitate form done also choose to wear a bracelet saying this made by companies chosen by the state a doctor can help get. The M.O.S.T. form often is on paper with bits of red and the Do Not Resuscitate form often is on solid yellow paper.

HIPAA Permits Disclosure of MOST to Other Health Care Professionals as Necessary

Medical Orders for Scope of Treatment (MOST)

This is a Physician Order Sheet based on the patient's medical condition and wishes. Any section not completed indicates full treatment for that section. **When the need occurs, first follow these orders, then contact physician.**

Patient's Last Name:	Effective Date of Form:
Patient's First Name, Middle Initial:	Patient's Date of Birth:

Section A — Check One Box Only

CARDIOPULMONARY RESUSCITATION (CPR): Patient has no pulse and is not breathing.

- ○ Attempt Resuscitation (CPR)
- ○ Do Not Attempt Resuscitation (DNR/no CPR)

When not in cardiopulmonary arrest, follow orders in **B, C,** and **D**.

Section B — Check One Box Only

MEDICAL INTERVENTIONS: Patient has pulse and/or is breathing.

- ○ **Full Scope of Treatment:** Use intubation, advanced airway interventions, mechanical ventilation, cardioversion as indicated, medical treatment, IV fluids, etc.; also provide comfort measures. **Transfer to hospital if indicated.**
- ○ **Limited Additional Interventions:** Use medical treatment, IV fluids and cardiac monitoring as indicated. Do not use intubation or mechanical ventilation. May consider use of less invasive airway support such as BiPAP or CPAP. Also provide comfort measures. **Transfer to hospital if indicated. Avoid intensive care.**
- ○ **Comfort Measures:** Keep clean, warm and dry. Use medication by any route, positioning, wound care and other measures to relieve pain and suffering. Use oxygen, suction and manual treatment of airway obstruction as needed for comfort. **Do not transfer to hospital** unless comfort needs cannot be met in current location.

Other Instructions: _____

Section C — Check One Box Only

ANTIBIOTICS

- ○ Antibiotics if indicated
- ○ Determine use or limitation of antibiotics when infection occurs
- ○ No Antibiotics (use other measures to relieve symptoms)

Other Instructions: _____

Section D — Check One Box Only in Each Column

MEDICALLY ADMINISTERED FLUIDS AND NUTRITION: Offer oral fluids and nutrition if physically feasible.

- ☐ IV fluids if indicated
- ☐ IV fluids for a defined trial period
- ☐ No IV fluids (provide other measures to ensure comfort)
- ☐ Feeding tube long-term if indicated
- ☐ Feeding tube for a defined trial period
- ☐ No feeding tube

Other Instructions: _____

Section E — Check the Appropriate Box

DISCUSSED WITH AND AGREED TO BY:

- ☐ Patient
- ☐ Parent or guardian if patient is a minor
- ☐ Health care agent
- ☐ Legal guardian of the patient
- ☐ Attorney-in-fact with power to make health care decisions
- ☐ Spouse
- ☐ Majority of patient's reasonably available parents and adult children
- ☐ Majority of patient's reasonably available adult siblings
- ☐ An individual with an established relationship with the patient who is acting in good faith and can reliably convey the wishes of the patient

Basis for order must be documented in medical record.

MD/DO, PA, or NP Name (Print):	MD/DO, PA, or NP Signature and Date (Required):	Phone #:

Signature of Patient, Parent of Minor, Guardian, Health Care Agent, Spouse, or Other Personal Representative
(Signature is required and must either be on this form or on file)

I agree that adequate information has been provided and significant thought has been given to life-prolonging measures. Treatment preferences have been expressed to the physician (MD/DO), physician assistant, or nurse practitioner. This document reflects those treatment preferences and indicates informed consent.
If signed by a patient representative, preferences expressed must reflect patient's wishes as best understood by that representative. Contact information for personal representative should be provided on the back of this form.
You are not required to sign this form to receive treatment.

Patient or Representative Name (Print):	Patient or Representative Signature:	Relationship (write "self" if patient):

Send Form with Patient/Resident when Transferred or Discharged

HIPAA Permits Disclosure of MOST to Other Health Care Professionals as Necessary

Contact Information

Patient Representative:	Relationship:	Phone#: Cell Phone #:	
Health Care Professional Preparing Form:	Preparer Title:	Preferred Phone#:	Date Prepared:

Directions for Completing Form

Completing MOST

- MOST must be reviewed and prepared by a health care professional in consultation with the patient or patient representative.
- MOST is a medical order and must be signed and dated by a licensed physician (MD/DO), physician assistant, or nurse practitioner to be valid. **Be sure to document the basis for the order in the progress notes of the medical record.** Mode of communication (e.g., in person, by telephone, etc.) also should be documented.
- The signature of the patient or his/her representative is required; however, if the patient's representative is not reasonably available to sign the original form, a copy of the completed form with the signature of the patient's representative must be placed in the medical record and "on file" must be written in the appropriate signature field on the front of this form or in the review section below.
- Use of original form is required. **Be sure to send the original form with the patient.**
- MOST is part of advance care planning, which also may include a living will and health care power of attorney
- (HCPOA). If there is a HCPOA, living will, or other advance directive, a copy should be attached if available. **MOST may suspend any conflicting directions in a patient's previously executed HCPOA, living will, or other advance directive.**
- **There is no requirement that a patient have a MOST.**
- MOST is recognized under N. C. Gen. Stat. 90-21.17

Reviewing MOST

Review of the MOST form is recommended when:
- The patient is admitted to and/or discharged from a health care facility; or
- There is a substantial change in the patient's health status.

This MOST must be reviewed if:
- The patient's treatment preferences change.

If MOST is revised or becomes invalid, draw a line through Sections A - E and write "VOID" in large letters.

Revocation of MOST

A patient with capacity or the patient's representative (if the patient lacks capacity) can revoke the MOST at any time and request alternative treatment based on the known preferences of the patient or, if unknown, the patient's best interests.

Review of MOST

Review Date	Reviewer and location of review	MD/DO, PA, or NP Signature (required)	Signature of patient or representative (preferred)	Outcome of Review
				○ No Change ○ FORM VOIDED, new form completed ○ FORM VOIDED, no new form
				○ No Change ○ FORM VOIDED, new form completed ○ FORM VOIDED, no new form
				○ No Change ○ FORM VOIDED, new form completed ○ FORM VOIDED, no new form
				○ No Change ○ FORM VOIDED, new form completed ○ FORM VOIDED, no new form
				○ No Change ○ FORM VOIDED, new form completed ○ FORM VOIDED, no new form

Send Form with Patient/Resident when Transferred or Discharged

DO NOT ALTER THIS FORM!

NC DEPARTMENT OF HEALTH AND HUMAN SERVICES

Division of Health Service Regulation • Office of Emergency Medical Services
www.ncdhhs.gov/dhsr/EMS/ems.htm • NCDHHS is an equal opportunity employer and provider. • 03/2024

PAGE INTENTIONALLY LEFT BLANK

Effective Date: _____

Expiration Date, if any: _____

☐ **Check box if no expiration**

DO NOT RESUSCITATE ORDER

Patient's full name: _____

In the event of cardiac and/or pulmonary arrest of the patient, efforts at cardiopulmonary resuscitation of the patient SHOULD NOT be initiated. This order does not affect other medically indicated and comfort care.

I have documented the basis for this order and the consent required by the NC General Statute 90-21.17(b) in the patient's records.

_____
Signature of Attending Physician/Physician Assistant/Nurse Practitioner

_____
Printed Name of Attending Physician

_____
Address

_____
City, State, Zip

Telephone Number (office) _____

Telephone Number (emergency) _____

Do Not Copy   Do Not Alter

Division of Health Service Regulation • Office of Emergency Medical Services
www.ncdhhs.gov/dhsr/EMS/ems.htm • NCDHHS is an equal opportunity employer and provider. • 03/2024

CHAPTER 14
FORM 8: STATUTORY SHORT FORM POWER OF ATTORNEY

FORM LETS PERSON GIVE POWER OVER THEIR PROPERTY AND MONEY
This form lets power be given to someone to let them do things to help. Many people call this form a "Financial Power Of Attorney". The form is called "statutory" since it is found in state law statutes for people to use if wanted, and is called "short" since it is very short and easy to use compared to similar forms used. This form is a statutory form found in law at N. C. General Statutes § 32C-3-301.

FORM GIVES POWER TO LET SOMEONE HELP WITH PROPERTY AND MONEY
This form lets a person (called in the form the "Principal") give power to someone (called in the form the "Agent" or "Attorney-in-Fact") to do things involving the Principal's money and property and other things. This form can let the Agent for the Principal pay bills, move money in accounts, buy or sell items, sign contracts, borrow, and get information from various places. Often the Agent is a trusted person like spouse, relative, or close friend. The form can help if a person is sick, busy, or away, and may avoid need for court action or nursing home. A person till incapacitated can still act like normal, and can overrule or fire an Agent. The form is "durable" which means it still works if the Principal is incapacitated but power ends at their death.

PEOPLE CAN SELECT POWERS AND WRITE INSTRUCTIONS
In the main part of the form a person must initial to say which powers are given, or they can initial the last item to give all the listed powers. Many people in the Grant Of General Authority part do give all these powers since if an Agent's power is not clear a bank or other party may delay or not obey the Agent at all. But most people do not give the powers in the Grant Of Specific Authority part since these powers are less often needed and are riskier. Instructions can be written but many people skip this to not risk legal issues.

DUE TO RISKS INCLUDING FRAUD MANY SKIP THIS FORM
Doing this form can be risky since an Agent can do bad things like steal, waste money, or be careless. Agents have a "fiduciary duty" to use due care and act in "best interests" of a person, so they can be sued later, but later they may be out of money. Usually banks or others can't be blamed for obeying an Agent. This area of law is complex and basic acts may be fine for an Agent to do like paying bills, moving funds, requesting records, or signing contracts that help the Principal. But less usual acts may be improper like as a gift handing money or property to the Principal's or Agent's family or friends, making risky investments, or doing things that are at all unusual. Some people before using this form first ask a lawyer for advice.

SIGN FORM WITH A NOTARY
To be valid a person signs the form in front of a notary who notarizes it. The completed form can be kept by a person till needed, or it can be given immediately to the Agent to hold and use if ever it is needed. Some people quickly show the form to a bank or other places to try to make clear it should be followed later. To cancel the form a person can tell the Agent and take back copies, and maybe tell everyone who saw it. Note, a bank or other party may much later ask for an "Agent's Certification", and this is the form's last page.

NORTH CAROLINA
STATUTORY SHORT FORM POWER OF ATTORNEY

NOTICE: THE POWERS GRANTED BY THIS DOCUMENT ARE BROAD AND SWEEPING. THEY ARE DEFINED IN CHAPTER 32C OF THE NORTH CAROLINA GENERAL STATUTES, WHICH EXPRESSLY PERMITS THE USE OF ANY OTHER OR DIFFERENT FORM OF POWER OF ATTORNEY DESIRED BY THE PARTIES CONCERNED.

IMPORTANT INFORMATION

This power of attorney authorizes another person (your agent) to make decisions concerning your property for you (the principal). Your agent will be able to make decisions and act with respect to your property (including your money) whether or not you are able to act for yourself. The meaning of authority over subjects listed on this form is explained in the North Carolina Uniform Power of Attorney Act.

This power of attorney does **not** authorize the agent to make health-care decisions for you.

You should select someone you trust to serve as your agent. Unless you specify otherwise, generally the agent's authority will continue until you die or revoke the power of attorney or the agent resigns or is unable to act for you.

Your agent is entitled to reasonable compensation unless you state otherwise in the Additional Provisions and Exclusions.

This form provides for designation of one agent, a successor agent, and a second successor agent. If you wish to name more than one agent, successor agent, and second successor agent, you may name a coagent, successor coagent, or second successor coagent in the Additional Provisions and Exclusions. Coagents, successor coagents, or second successor coagents are not required to act together unless you include that requirement in the Additional Provisions and Exclusions.

If your agent is unable or unwilling to act for you, your power of attorney will end unless you have named a successor agent. You may also name a second successor agent.

This power of attorney becomes effective immediately.

If you have questions about the power of attorney or the authority you are granting to your agent, you should seek legal advice before signing this form.

DESIGNATION OF AGENT

I, _____, name the following person as my agent:
          (Name of Principal)

Name of Agent: _____

This power of attorney is <u>durable</u> and shall not be affected by my subsequent incapacity or mental incompetence or by passage or lapse of time, unless specified otherwise in this document.

DESIGNATION OF SUCCESSOR AGENT(S) (OPTIONAL)

If my agent is unable or unwilling to act for me, I name as my successor agent:

Name of Successor Agent: _____

If my successor agent is unable or unwilling to act, I name as second successor agent:

Name of Second Successor Agent: _____

INITIAL below if you want to give an agent the power to name a successor agent.

(_____) I give to my acting agent the full power to appoint another to act as my agent, and full power to revoke such appointment, if no agent named by me above is willing or able to act.

GRANT OF GENERAL AUTHORITY

I grant my agent and any successor agent general authority to act for me with respect to the following subjects as defined in the North Carolina Uniform Power of Attorney Act, Chapter 32C of the General Statutes:

(INITIAL each subject you want to include in the agent's general authority. If you wish to grant general authority over all the subjects you may initial just "All Preceding Subjects")

(_____) Real Property
(_____) Tangible Personal Property
(_____) Stocks and Bonds
(_____) Commodities and Options
(_____) Banks and Other Financial Institutions
(_____) Operation of Entity
(_____) Insurance and Annuities
(_____) Estates, Trusts, and Other Beneficial Interests
(_____) Claims and Litigation
(_____) Personal and Family Maintenance
(_____) Benefits from Governmental Programs or Civil or Military Service
(_____) Retirement Plans
(_____) Taxes
(_____) All Preceding Subjects

GRANT OF SPECIFIC AUTHORITY (OPTIONAL)

My agent MAY NOT do any of the following specific acts for me UNLESS I have INITIALED the specific authority listed below:

(CAUTION: Granting any of the following will give your agent the authority to take actions that could significantly reduce your property or change how your property is distributed at your death. INITIAL ONLY the specific authority you WANT to give your agent.)

(____) Make a gift, subject to the limitations provided in G.S. 32C-2-217

(____) Create or change rights of survivorship

(____) Create or change a beneficiary designation

(____) Authorize another person to use the authority granted under this power of attorney

(____) Waive my right to be a beneficiary of a joint and survivor annuity, including a survivor benefit under a retirement plan

(____) Exercise fiduciary powers that I have authority to delegate

(____) Disclaim or refuse an interest in property, including a power of appointment

(____) Access the content of electronic communications

EXERCISE OF SPECIFIC AUTHORITY IN FAVOR OF AGENT (OPTIONAL)

(____) UNLESS INITIALED, my agent MAY NOT exercise any of the grants of specific authority initialed above in favor of the agent or an individual to whom the agent owes a legal obligation of support.

ADDITIONAL PROVISIONS AND EXCLUSIONS (OPTIONAL)

(____) _____

_____

_____

_____

_____

_____

_____

_____

_____

_____

EFFECTIVE DATE

This power of attorney is effective immediately.

NOMINATION OF GUARDIAN (OPTIONAL)

INITIAL below ONLY if you WANT your acting agent to be your Guardian.

(____) If it becomes necessary for a court to appoint a guardian of my estate or a general guardian, I nominate my agent acting under this power of attorney to be the guardian to serve without bond or other security.

RELIANCE ON THIS POWER OF ATTORNEY

Any person, including my agent, may rely upon the validity of this power of attorney or a copy of it unless that person knows it has terminated or is invalid.

MEANING AND EFFECT

The meaning and effect of this power of attorney shall for all purposes be determined by the law of the State of North Carolina.

SIGNATURE AND ACKNOWLEDGEMENT

_____   _____
Your Signature   Date

_____
Your Name Printed

State of _____, County of _____

I certify that the following person personally appeared before me this day, acknowledging to me that he or she signed the foregoing document: _____.

Date: _____   _____
                              Signature of Notary Public

(Official Seal)   _____, Notary Public
                              Printed or typed name

                              My commission expires: _____

IMPORTANT INFORMATION FOR AGENT

Agent's Duties

When you accept the authority granted under this power of attorney, a special legal relationship is created between you and the principal. This relationship imposes upon you legal duties that continue until you resign or your authority is terminated or the power of attorney is terminated or revoked. You must:

1. Do what you know the principal reasonably expects you to do with the principal's property or, if you do not know the principal's expectations, act in the principal's best interest;
2. Act in good faith;
3. Do nothing beyond the authority granted in this power of attorney; and
4. Disclose your identity as an agent whenever you act for the principal by writing or printing the name of the principal and signing your own name as "agent" in the following manner: (Principal's Name) by (Your Signature) as Agent.

Unless the Additional Provisions and Exclusions in this power of attorney state otherwise, you must also:

1. Act loyally for the principal's benefit;
2. Avoid conflicts that would impair your ability to act in the principal's best interest;
3. Act with care, competence, and diligence;
4. Keep a record of all receipts, disbursements, and transactions made on behalf of principal;
5. Cooperate with any person that has authority to make health care decisions for the principal to do what you know the principal reasonably expects, or if you do not know the principal's expectations, to act in the principal's best interest;
6. Attempt to preserve the principal's estate plan if you know the plan and preserving the plan is consistent with the principal's best interest; and
7. Account to the principal (or a person designated by the principal (if any)) in the Additional Provisions and Exclusions.

Termination of Agent's Authority

You must stop acting on behalf of the principal if you learn of any event that terminated or revoked this power of attorney or your authority under this power of attorney. Events that terminate a power of attorney or your authority to act under a power of attorney include:

1. Death of the principal;
2. The principal's revocation of the power of attorney or the termination of your authority;
3. The occurrence of a termination event stated in the power of attorney;
4. The purpose of the power of attorney is fully accomplished;
5. If you are married to the principal, your divorce from the principal, unless the Additional Provisions and Exclusions in this power of attorney state that your divorce from the principal will not terminate your authority; or
6. A guardian of the principal's estate or the principal's general guardian revokes the power of attorney or terminates your authority.

Liability of Agent

The meaning of the authority granted to you is defined in the North Carolina Uniform Power of Attorney Act as set forth in Chapter 32C of the North Carolina General Statutes. If you violate the North Carolina Uniform Power of Attorney Act or act outside the authority granted, you may be liable for any damages caused by your violation.

If there is anything about this document or your duties that you do not understand, you should seek legal advice.

AGENT'S CERTIFICATION AS TO THE VALIDITY OF POWER OF ATTORNEY AND AGENT'S AUTHORITY

(G.S. 32C-3-302; OPTIONAL FORM TO LATER BE USED BY AGENT)

I, _____ (Name of Agent), do hereby state and affirm the following under penalty of perjury:

(1) _____ (Name of Principal) granted me authority as an agent or successor agent in a power of attorney dated _____.

(2) The powers and authority granted to me in the power of attorney are currently exercisable by me.

(3) I have no actual knowledge of any of the following:
(a) The principal is deceased.
(b) The power of attorney or my authority as agent under the power of attorney has been revoked or terminated, partially or otherwise.
(c) The principal lacked the understanding and capacity to make and communicate decisions regarding his estate and person at the time the power of attorney was executed.
(d) The power of attorney was not properly executed and is not a legal, valid power of attorney.
(e) (Insert other relevant statements)
_____
_____
_____
_____
_____

(4) I agree not to exercise any powers granted under the power of attorney if I become aware that the principal is deceased, that the power of attorney has been revoked or terminated, or that my authority as agent under the power of attorney has been revoked or terminated.

SIGNATURE AND ACKNOWLEDGMENT

_____   _____
Agent's Signature   Date

_____   _____
Agent's Name Printed   Agent's Telephone Number

_____
Agent's Address

COUNTY OF _____, STATE OF _____.

Date: _____   _____
                                              Signature of Notary Public

(Official Seal)
                                   _____, Notary Public
                                              Printed or typed name
                                              My commission expires: _____

CHAPTER 15
FORM 9: AUTHORIZATION TO CONSENT TO HEALTH CARE FOR MINOR

FORM LETS PARENT GIVE POWER TO PERSON OVER CHILD'S HEALTH CARE

This form lets a parent give power over health care of a child under 18 to the person named in the form. This form is a statutory form found in state law at N. C. General Statutes § 32A-34.

FORM GIVES POWER OVER CHILD'S HEALTH CARE TO SOMEONE

The form lets a parent give power over health care of a child under 18 to a person. This form is often used if parent is away from a child for weeks or several times a week due to work, school, training, prison, recreation, sports or academic camp, or family visits. Often given power in the form is a relative like aunt or grandparent, a friend watching a child, or a teacher or coach. Using this form may avoid need for legal action like a change in custody. Usually the person given power can be overruled or fired by the parent. The form is usually not used for small things like a night with babysitter, weekend with relatives, or daycare. This form giving power over health care is often enough but some parents also do a Power of Attorney form and write in a child's name and say power is given over school, discipline, housing, food, and health care.

PEOPLE MUST SIGN FORM USING A NOTARY

The form must be signed by a custodial parent while with a person who is notary who then notarizes and signs it. Some people modify the form to have 2 custodial parents sign to make the form seem more persuasive to schools, doctors, and others. People can keep the form till needed or hand it out to the person named in it. Some cautious people quickly in person show the form to schools or medical people to get them to understand it should be followed later.

AUTHORIZATION TO CONSENT TO HEALTH CARE FOR MINOR

(N. C. General Statutes § 32A-34)

I, _____, of _____ County, North Carolina, am the custodial parent having legal custody of _____, a minor child, age _____, born _____, 20____.

I authorize _____, an adult in whose care the minor child has been entrusted, and who resides at _____ _____, to do any acts which may be necessary or proper to provide for the health care of the minor child, including, but not limited to, the power (i) to provide for such health care at any hospital or other institution, or the employing of any physician, dentist, nurse, or other person whose services may be needed for such health care, and (ii) to consent to and authorize any health care, including administration of anesthesia, X-ray examination, performance of operations, and other procedures by physicians, dentists, and other medical personnel except the withholding or withdrawal of life sustaining procedures.

[Optional: This consent shall be effective from the date of execution to and including _____, 20____].

By signing here, I indicate that I have the understanding and capacity to communicate health care decisions and that I am fully informed as to the contents of this document and understand the full import of this grant of powers to the agent named herein.

_____   _____
Custodial Parent   Date

STATE OF NORTH CAROLINA
COUNTY OF _____

On this _____ day of _____, 20___, personally appeared before me the named _____, to me known and known to me to be the person described in and who executed the foregoing instrument and he (or she) acknowledges that he (or she) executed the same and being duly sworn by me, made oath that the statements in the foregoing instrument are true.

(OFFICIAL SEAL)

_____
Notary Public
My Commission Expires: _____

CHAPTER 16
FORM 10: AUTHORIZATION ABOUT BODILY REMAINS

LETS AGENT BE NAMED OR INSTRUCTIONS GIVEN ABOUT DEAD BODY

This form lets a person give instructions about what to do with their dead body and related matters, and name someone to control these things. In North Carolina this can also be done in other legal documents like a Will, Health Care Power of Attorney, Preneed Funeral Control, or Cremation form.

IN FORM PERSON CAN BE NAMED AGENT TO BE IN CHARGE

In the form a person can be named to be "Authorizing Agent" to later control disposition of the dead body, funeral, cremation, and related matters. If this form is not done by law control is by closest family (in order this is any spouse, adult child, parents, brothers/sisters, and then others). In reality people rarely remove family from power, like only if they may be too upset while mourning, waste money, or do unwanted things. Payment for things comes from any pre-paid funeral accounts, insurance, and the dead person's money and property, and Executor and family legally must help arrange payment. People including family should do the funeral, burial, ceremonies, and related things a person wanted if their money and property left can afford it.

IN FORM CAN GIVE INSTRUCTIONS FOR FUNERAL AND BODY

The form has room to write instructions that everyone should follow but many people skip this and trust family or person given power to be wise or do what was discussed. People often skip naming a person but write long instructions that later everyone legally must follow. Some people write simple things, like they write to ask for "Direct Burial" or "Direct Cremation" (this is cheap and done without delay or family watching).

TO COMPLETE FORM SIGN WITH 2 WITNESSES

The form should be signed by a person with 2 witnesses at least 18 who also sign. The form should be kept so it is found soon after death (like within hours) or it can be given immediately to a person to hold on to.

AUTHORIZATION ABOUT BODILY REMAINS

I, _____, of _____, North Carolina, pursuant to North Carolina General Statutes § 130A-420 and other laws do name _____ as my Authorizing Agent with power to control disposition of my dead body including cremation.

I give these instructions about the place, type, method of disposition, and other instructions concerning my dead body:

_____

_____

_____

_____

_____

_____

_____

_____

_____

_____

_____

_____

_____

_____

Signature:_____

Witness:_____   Witness:_____

APPENDIX:
SAMPLE FILLED OUT LEGAL FORMS

TO GET FORMS TO USE PEOPLE CAN:
   (1) PHOTOCOPY BOOK PAGES,
   (2) TEAR OUT PAGES FROM A BOOK, OR
   (3) DOWNLOAD BOOK WITH FORMS FROM WWW.DAVENPORTPUBLISHING.COM,
   AND USUALLY USING PDF FORM IS BEST TO AVOID SPACING/FORMAT CHANGES.

EMAIL ANY COMMENTS TO DAVENPORTPRESS@GMAIL.COM.

On the next pages to show how it can be done are some sample filled out legal forms.

People can add words to legal forms by computer or typewriter to be neater, but many people just by hand use pen, marker, or pencil to handwrite words into forms.

It is not required but better if signatures and dates are in ink or marker (not pencil).

Many parts of the forms especially spaces for Will gifts can be left empty and unfilled.

Anyone can fill in the words in a legal form not just the person doing the form, like a friend with neat writing can fill in all the words, addresses, and dates that are needed. Only the signatures must be done by each person doing the form for themselves.

When adding words in a form any of these is a fine way to do this:
        "I appoint ___*John Doe*___ as Agent",
        "I appoint ___John Doe___ as Agent",
        "I appoint John Doe as Agent".

When doing forms it may help to know "respectively" means "in the order just stated".

People need not worry about neatness or small mistakes, and a document is usually fine if those people who knew person during their life can tell the likely meaning.

Sample Filled Out Form: Will (Standard)
with Gifts section skipped to not bother making small gifts

LAST WILL AND TESTAMENT

I, __Paul Samuel Maxwell__, of __Forsyth County__, North Carolina, do revoke all prior Wills and testamentary documents and do make, publish, and declare this as my Will. I am of sound mind and under no duress or undue influence and act voluntarily.

1. LIVING SPOUSE AND CHILDREN. To show I am mentally fit and have sufficient memory to do a Will I do say I now have the following living spouse and living children:
_____ none _____
_____.

2. GIFTS. I give these gifts in this Will, but to get a gift in this section the recipient must survive me except as otherwise stated below.

I give _____ to _____.
I give _____ to _____.
I give _____ to _____.
I give _____ to _____.
I give _____ to _____.
I give _____ to _____.
I give _____ to _____.
I give _____ to _____.
I give _____ to _____.
I give _____ to _____.
I give _____ to _____.

SKIPPED (written across the gifts section)

3. RESIDUE. The rest, residue, and remainder of my estate, and anything else, I give:

a) to __Susan Maxwell__ who survive me and with persons just named who survive me taking the share of non-survivors, then if anything remains

b) to __Oscar Adam Maxwell and Mary Ann Tabor__ and if any of those just now named do not survive me their part goes to their lineal descendants per stirpes.

59

4. ADMINISTRATION. I name, nominate, and appoint <u>*Susan Maxwell my sister*</u> as Personal Representative including for me, my Will, and my estate.

5. MISCELLANEOUS. The following applies to this Will and generally.

In this Will no part left unfilled is a mistake including spaces in the residue clause.

The facts support and I want North Carolina law to apply to this Will and my estate.

I order that my just debts, funeral and related expenses, and taxes be paid as soon after my death as practical but only those items my Personal Representative chooses to pay.

Priority of Will gifts of the same type is based on the order they are made in this Will.

The words give and gift also means a devise, bequest, grant, legacy, or similar.

I am intentionally not providing by Will or other ways for some family, including I am not providing for some children of mine and also children of a deceased child of mine.

If a Will gift reasonably mentions survival then survival is an absolute condition and anti-lapse laws or similar provisions have no effect and without survival the gift lapses. Unless a Will gift specifies otherwise if a Will gift goes to multiple recipients if any do not survive me the part to them lapses and instead goes to other surviving recipients.

No earlier transfer reduces a Will gift unless I usually called it a loan or advancement.

In this Will any gendered word includes all genders, and the singular includes the plural and vice versa, and they can mean a single person or many persons.

Unless a Will specifically says otherwise a secured debt including a mortgage or lien shall not be paid off including by a Personal Representative or in probate, and a recipient of a Will gift of property takes it subject to debts. Also, no recipient of property who may lose it or who pays to keep it may have my estate or others pay or do exoneration.

If I somehow lost ownership of an item in a specific Will gift the gift is extinguished.

I request and authorize any informal, summary, and quick probate or similar action. Any Personal Representative may act independently with no supervision of any court, including independent administration, and with no inventory, appraisal, or other action.

I give any Personal Representative the a) fullest authority, discretion, and powers allowed by state law, b) power to lease, sell, mortgage, convey, or keep property including real property in a manner and time they deem helpful or proper, and c) authority to settle or pay claims or debts in the time and manner they choose. Any Personal Representative or other fiduciary shall have all powers and authorities that may be given by statute or common law in any jurisdiction they may act, including under North Carolina law.

Any Guardian of any type, Conservator, Custodian, or other person managing a minor's property or money may use or invade the principal and sell property without court action.

If context permits the terms Personal Representative and Executor and Administrator are interchangeable, Conservator and Guardian of the Estate and Guardian of Property and Custodian are interchangeable, and residue and residuary are interchangeable. Any such person may stand in the place of and have all powers like the others named here.

The residue includes lapsed or failed gifts, insurance paid to the estate, digital assets, inheritances owed me, and all I had power of appointment or testamentary disposition over.

Any Personal Representative may access, manage, delete, modify, transfer, and otherwise control any digital accounts and assets I had any interest in or power over.

Any Personal Representative, Executor, Administrator, Guardian of any type like for a person or estate, Conservator, Custodian, and any other fiduciary under this Will or otherwise shall qualify and serve without bond, surety, security, surety bond, or similar.

If evidence does not show it likely a person survived me by 120 hours (5 days) then for this Will and my estate they shall be deemed in all ways as having died before me.

If part of this Will is by law invalid or unenforceable other provisions remain in effect.

Any Personal Representative may at any time transfer money or property of a minor under age 18 to a Custodian to act under the North Carolina Uniform Transfers to Minors Act or similar law anywhere, and may pick a person to be Custodian including themselves.

TESTATOR

IN WITNESS WHEREOF, I, _Paul Samuel Maxwell_, the Testator, sign my name to this instrument this, and do hereby declare that I sign and execute this instrument as my Will and that I sign it willingly, that I execute it as my free and voluntary act for the purposes therein expressed, and that I am 18 years of age or older, of sound mind, and under no constraint or undue influence.

Paul Samuel Maxwell
Signature of Testator

WITNESSES

We, _Susan Ann Moon_ and _Eve Mable Smith_, the Witnesses, sign our names to this instrument, and do hereby declare that the Testator signs and executes this instrument as the Will of the Testator in our presence and that the Testator signs it willingly, and that each of us at the request of the Testator and in the presence and hearing of the Testator, and in the presence and hearing of each other, hereby signs this Will to function legally as witness to the Testator's signing, and to the best of our knowledge the Testator is eighteen years of age or older, of sound mind, and under no constraint or undue influence.

Susan Ann Moon   _14 2nd Street, Greensboro, NC 27203_
Signature of Witness #1   Address of Witness #1

Eve Mable Smith   _35 Buffalo Road, Denver, Colorado 80101_
Signature of Witness #2   Address of Witness #2

Sample Filled Out Form: Will (Guardian)
with many gifts written in Gifts section, Guardian Clause used, and Residue Clause using percentages

LAST WILL AND TESTAMENT

I, __Paul Brian Baker__ of __Durham County__, North Carolina, do revoke all prior Wills and testamentary documents and do make, publish, and declare this as my Will. I am of sound mind and under no duress or undue influence and act voluntarily.

1. LIVING SPOUSE AND CHILDREN. To show I am mentally fit and have sufficient memory to do a Will I do say I now have the following living spouse and living children:

__Ruth May Baker wife__ __Oscar Elliot Baker young son__
__Karen Lisa Lundy daughter__ __Derek Rupert Baker son__.

2. GIFTS. I give these gifts in this Will, but to get a gift in this section the recipient must survive me except as otherwise stated below.

I give __big oak table__ to __Anne J. Smith__.

I give __$5,000 and Ford Truck__ to __Loretta Marsha Baxter__.

I give __buildings, land, and fixtures at 63 Wentworth Road, Budd, North Carolina__, to __Kenneth Alan Ford__.

I give __all real property and fixtures I own in Wake County in North Carolina__ to __Amy Marie Fox and Pamela Sue Fox__.

I give __903 Iceberg Road, Anchorage, Alaska__ to __James Eric Hanson__.

I give __Irish jewelry and my wedding ring__ to __Mary Natalie Swanson__.

I give __all jewelry not given above__ to __Kay Baxter and Mary Baxter__.

I give __$781.35__ to __Mary Natalie Swanson and Kevin Kilby__.

I give __Wells Fargo acct ending in #8923__ to __Lawrence Deer a hunting buddy__.

I give __all spare tires and auto parts__ to __Victor Perez my mechanic__.

3. RESIDUE. The rest, residue, and remainder of my estate, and anything else, I give:

a) to __Ruth May Baker__ who survive me and with persons just named who survive me taking the share of non-survivors, then if anything remains

b) to __50% to Oscar Elliot Baker, 35% to Karen Lisa Lundy, 5% to Mary Sue Baker, and 10% to Luis Sanchez my friend__ and if any of those just now named do not survive me their part goes to their lineal descendants per stirpes.

4. ADMINISTRATION. I name, nominate, and appoint __Ruth May Baker__ as Personal Representative including for me, my Will, and my estate.

5. GUARDIAN. I name Amanda Sue Brubaker my sister to be Guardian Of The Person of any minor child of mine and to have care, authority, custody, and other control of them. I name this same person to be Guardian Of The Estate for any minor child and to have care, control, and power over their property, money, and estate.

6. MISCELLANEOUS. The following applies to this Will and generally.

In this Will no part left unfilled is a mistake including spaces in the residue clause.

The facts support and I want North Carolina law to apply to this Will and my estate.

I order that my just debts, funeral and related expenses, and taxes be paid as soon after my death as practical but only those items my Personal Representative chooses to pay.

Priority of Will gifts of the same type is based on the order they are made in this Will.

The words give and gift also means a devise, bequest, grant, legacy, or similar.

I am intentionally not providing by Will or other ways for some family, including I am not providing for some children of mine and also children of a deceased child of mine.

If a Will gift reasonably mentions survival then survival is an absolute condition and anti-lapse laws or similar provisions have no effect and without survival the gift lapses. Unless a Will gift specifies otherwise if a Will gift goes to multiple recipients if any do not survive me the part to them lapses and instead goes to other surviving recipients.

No earlier transfer reduces a Will gift unless I usually called it a loan or advancement.

In this Will any gendered word includes all genders, and the singular includes the plural and vice versa, and they can mean a single person or many persons.

Unless a Will specifically says otherwise a secured debt including a mortgage or lien shall not be paid off including by a Personal Representative or in probate, and a recipient of a Will gift of property takes it subject to debts. Also, no recipient of property who may lose it or who pays to keep it may have my estate or others pay or do exoneration.

If I somehow lost ownership of an item in a specific Will gift the gift is extinguished.

I request and authorize any informal, summary, and quick probate or similar action. Any Personal Representative may act independently with no supervision of any court, including independent administration, and with no inventory, appraisal, or other action.

I give any Personal Representative the a) fullest authority, discretion, and powers allowed by state law, b) power to lease, sell, mortgage, convey, or keep property including real property in a manner and time they deem helpful or proper, and c) authority to settle or pay claims or debts in the time and manner they choose. Any Personal Representative or other fiduciary shall have all powers and authorities that may be given by statute or common law in any jurisdiction they may act, including under North Carolina law.

Any Guardian of any type, Conservator, Custodian, or other person managing a minor's property or money may use or invade the principal and sell property without court action.

If context permits the terms Personal Representative and Executor and Administrator

are interchangeable, Conservator and Guardian of the Estate and Guardian of Property and Custodian are interchangeable, and residue and residuary are interchangeable. Any such person may stand in the place of and have all powers like the others named here.

The residue includes lapsed or failed gifts, insurance paid to the estate, digital assets, inheritances owed me, and all I had power of appointment or testamentary disposition over.

Any Personal Representative may access, manage, delete, modify, transfer, and otherwise control any digital accounts and assets I had any interest in or power over.

Any Personal Representative, Executor, Administrator, Guardian of any type like for a person or estate, Conservator, Custodian, and any other fiduciary under this Will or otherwise shall qualify and serve without bond, surety, security, surety bond, or similar.

If evidence does not show it likely a person survived me by 120 hours (5 days) then for this Will and my estate they shall be deemed in all ways as having died before me.

If part of this Will is by law invalid or unenforceable other provisions remain in effect.

Any Personal Representative may at any time transfer money or property of a minor under age 18 to a Custodian to act under the North Carolina Uniform Transfers to Minors Act or similar law anywhere, and may pick a person to be Custodian including themselves.

TESTATOR

IN WITNESS WHEREOF, I, __Paul Brian Baker__ the Testator, sign my name to this instrument this, and do hereby declare that I sign and execute this instrument as my Will and that I sign it willingly, that I execute it as my free and voluntary act for the purposes therein expressed, and that I am 18 years of age or older, of sound mind, and under no constraint or undue influence.

Paul Brian Baker
Signature of Testator

WITNESSES

We, __Olivia Anna Paulson__ and __Matthew John Paulson__, the Witnesses, sign our names to this instrument, and do hereby declare that the Testator signs and executes this instrument as the Will of the Testator in our presence and that the Testator signs it willingly, and that each of us at the request of the Testator and in the presence and hearing of the Testator, and in the presence and hearing of each other, hereby signs this Will to function legally as witness to the Testator's signing, and to the best of our knowledge the Testator is eighteen years of age or older, of sound mind, and under no constraint or undue influence.

Olivia Anna Paulson   82 Forest Road, Charlotte, NC 28204
Signature of Witness #1   Address of Witness #1

Matthew John Paulson   82 Forest Road, Charlotte, NC 28204
Signature of Witness #2   Address of Witness #2

Sample Filled Out Form : Will (Guardian) with Gifts section left unused and, then, the Residue Clause done only using 2nd space so as to gift to all branches of person's descendants equally

LAST WILL AND TESTAMENT

I, __Thomas Roger Tedford__ of __Guilford County__, North Carolina, do revoke all prior Wills and testamentary documents and do make, publish, and declare this as my Will. I am of sound mind and under no duress or undue influence and act voluntarily.

1. LIVING SPOUSE AND CHILDREN. To show I am mentally fit and have sufficient memory to do a Will I do say I now have the following living spouse and living children:

__Mary Paula Tedford my daughter__   __Gina Lola Smith my daughter__

_____.

2. GIFTS. I give these gifts in this Will, but to get a gift in this section the recipient must survive me except as otherwise stated below.

I give _____ to _____.

I give _____ to _____.

I give _____ to _____.

I give _____ to _____.

I give _____ to _____.

I give _____ to _____.

I give _____ to _____.

I give _____ to _____.

3. RESIDUE. The rest, residue, and remainder of my estate, and anything else, I give:

  a) to _____ who survive me and with persons just named who survive me taking the share of non-survivors, then if anything remains

  b) to __Brian Alan Tedford my deceased son,__ __Mary Paula Tedford my daughter,__ __and Gina Lola Smith my daughter__ and if any of those just now named do not survive me their part goes to their lineal descendants per stirpes.

4. ADMINISTRATION. I name, nominate, and appoint ___Mary Paula Tedford___
as Personal Representative including for me, my Will, and my estate.

5. MISCELLANEOUS. The following applies to this Will and generally.

In this Will no part left unfilled is a mistake including spaces in the residue clause.

The facts support and I want North Carolina law to apply to this Will and my estate.

I order that my just debts, funeral and related expenses, and taxes be paid as soon after my death as practical but only those items my Personal Representative chooses to pay.

Priority of Will gifts of the same type is based on the order they are made in this Will.

The words give and gift also means a devise, bequest, grant, legacy, or similar.

I am intentionally not providing by Will or other ways for some family, including I am not providing for some children of mine and also children of a deceased child of mine.

If a Will gift reasonably mentions survival then survival is an absolute condition and anti-lapse laws or similar provisions have no effect and without survival the gift lapses. Unless a Will gift specifies otherwise if a Will gift goes to multiple recipients if any do not survive me the part to them lapses and instead goes to other surviving recipients.

No earlier transfer reduces a Will gift unless I usually called it a loan or advancement.

In this Will any gendered word includes all genders, and the singular includes the plural and vice versa, and they can mean a single person or many persons.

Unless a Will specifically says otherwise a secured debt including a mortgage or lien shall not be paid off including by a Personal Representative or in probate, and a recipient of a Will gift of property takes it subject to debts. Also, no recipient of property who may lose it or who pays to keep it may have my estate or others pay or do exoneration.

If I somehow lost ownership of an item in a specific Will gift the gift is extinguished.

I request and authorize any informal, summary, and quick probate or similar action. Any Personal Representative may act independently with no supervision of any court, including independent administration, and with no inventory, appraisal, or other action.

I give any Personal Representative the a) fullest authority, discretion, and powers allowed by state law, b) power to lease, sell, mortgage, convey, or keep property including real property in a manner and time they deem helpful or proper, and c) authority to settle or pay claims or debts in the time and manner they choose. Any Personal Representative or other fiduciary shall have all powers and authorities that may be given by statute or common law in any jurisdiction they may act, including under North Carolina law.

Any Guardian of any type, Conservator, Custodian, or other person managing a minor's property or money may use or invade the principal and sell property without court action.

If context permits the terms Personal Representative and Executor and Administrator are interchangeable, Conservator and Guardian of the Estate and Guardian of Property and Custodian are interchangeable, and residue and residuary are interchangeable. Any such person may stand in the place of and have all powers like the others named here.

The residue includes lapsed or failed gifts, insurance paid to the estate, digital assets,

inheritances owed me, and all I had power of appointment or testamentary disposition over.

Any Personal Representative may access, manage, delete, modify, transfer, and otherwise control any digital accounts and assets I had any interest in or power over.

Any Personal Representative, Executor, Administrator, Guardian of any type like for a person or estate, Conservator, Custodian, and any other fiduciary under this Will or otherwise shall qualify and serve without bond, surety, security, surety bond, or similar.

If evidence does not show it likely a person survived me by 120 hours (5 days) then for this Will and my estate they shall be deemed in all ways as having died before me.

If part of this Will is by law invalid or unenforceable other provisions remain in effect.

Any Personal Representative may at any time transfer money or property of a minor under age 18 to a Custodian to act under the North Carolina Uniform Transfers to Minors Act or similar law anywhere, and may pick a person to be Custodian including themselves.

TESTATOR

IN WITNESS WHEREOF, I, __Thomas Roger Tedford__ , the Testator, sign my name to this instrument this, and do hereby declare that I sign and execute this instrument as my Will and that I sign it willingly, that I execute it as my free and voluntary act for the purposes therein expressed, and that I am 18 years of age or older, of sound mind, and under no constraint or undue influence.

Thomas Roger Tedford
Signature of Testator

WITNESSES

We, __Maria Bonita Buena__ and __Richard Max West__ , the Witnesses, sign our names to this instrument, and do hereby declare that the Testator signs and executes this instrument as the Will of the Testator in our presence and that the Testator signs it willingly, and that each of us at the request of the Testator and in the presence and hearing of the Testator, and in the presence and hearing of each other, hereby signs this Will to function legally as witness to the Testator's signing, and to the best of our knowledge the Testator is eighteen years of age or older, of sound mind, and under no constraint or undue influence.

Maria Bonita Buena   101 Fox Rd., Apt. #35 Clayton, NC 27003
Signature of Witness #1   Address of Witness #1

Richard Max West   28 Miller Avenue, Pineville, NC 27361
Signature of Witness #2   Address of Witness #2

Sample Filled Out Form : Will (Standard) with Will modified to have a 1 Part Residue Clause

LAST WILL AND TESTAMENT

I, __John David Smith__ , of __Mecklenburg County__ , North Carolina, do revoke all prior Wills and testamentary documents and do make, publish, and declare this as my Will. I am of sound mind and under no duress or undue influence and act voluntarily.

1. LIVING SPOUSE AND CHILDREN. To show I am mentally fit and have sufficient memory to do a Will I do say I now have the following living spouse and living children: __my son Adam Michael Smith__ .

2. GIFTS. I give these gifts in this Will, but to get a gift in this section the recipient must survive me except as otherwise stated below.

I give __$200__ to __each of my nieces and nephews so about $2,800 in total__ .

I give __$400__ to __Garner Food Shelf in Raleigh, North Carolina by city hall__ .

I give __$340__ to __my old church Trinity Catholic Church in Pueblo, Colorado__ .

I give _____ to _____ .

I give _____ to _____ .

I give _____ to _____ .

I give _____ to _____ .

I give _____ to _____ .

I give _____ to _____ .

I give _____ to _____ .

I give _____ to _____ .

3. RESIDUE. The rest, residue, and remainder of my estate, and anything else, I give to: __Adam Michael Smith__ and __Judy Paula Ford__ who survive me and if any of those just named do not survive me their part goes to their lineal descendants per stirpes.

4. ADMINISTRATION. I name, nominate, and appoint Judy Paula Ford my sister
as Personal Representative including for me, my Will, and my estate.

5. MISCELLANEOUS. The following applies to this Will and generally.

In this Will no part left unfilled is a mistake including spaces in the residue clause.

The facts support and I want North Carolina law to apply to this Will and my estate.

I order that my just debts, funeral and related expenses, and taxes be paid as soon after my death as practical but only those items my Personal Representative chooses to pay.

Priority of Will gifts of the same type is based on the order they are made in this Will.

The words give and gift also means a devise, bequest, grant, legacy, or similar.

I am intentionally not providing by Will or other ways for some family, including I am not providing for some children of mine and also children of a deceased child of mine.

If a Will gift reasonably mentions survival then survival is an absolute condition and anti-lapse laws or similar provisions have no effect and without survival the gift lapses. Unless a Will gift specifies otherwise if a Will gift goes to multiple recipients if any do not survive me the part to them lapses and instead goes to other surviving recipients.

No earlier transfer reduces a Will gift unless I usually called it a loan or advancement.

In this Will any gendered word includes all genders, and the singular includes the plural and vice versa, and they can mean a single person or many persons.

Unless a Will specifically says otherwise a secured debt including a mortgage or lien shall not be paid off including by a Personal Representative or in probate, and a recipient of a Will gift of property takes it subject to debts. Also, no recipient of property who may lose it or who pays to keep it may have my estate or others pay or do exoneration.

If I somehow lost ownership of an item in a specific Will gift the gift is extinguished.

I request and authorize any informal, summary, and quick probate or similar action. Any Personal Representative may act independently with no supervision of any court, including independent administration, and with no inventory, appraisal, or other action.

I give any Personal Representative the a) fullest authority, discretion, and powers allowed by state law, b) power to lease, sell, mortgage, convey, or keep property including real property in a manner and time they deem helpful or proper, and c) authority to settle or pay claims or debts in the time and manner they choose. Any Personal Representative or other fiduciary shall have all powers and authorities that may be given by statute or common law in any jurisdiction they may act, including under North Carolina law.

Any Guardian of any type, Conservator, Custodian, or other person managing a minor's property or money may use or invade the principal and sell property without court action.

If context permits the terms Personal Representative and Executor and Administrator are interchangeable, Conservator and Guardian of the Estate and Guardian of Property and Custodian are interchangeable, and residue and residuary are interchangeable. Any such person may stand in the place of and have all powers like the others named here.

The residue includes lapsed or failed gifts, insurance paid to the estate, digital assets, inheritances owed me, and all I had power of appointment or testamentary disposition over.

Any Personal Representative may access, manage, delete, modify, transfer, and otherwise control any digital accounts and assets I had any interest in or power over.

Any Personal Representative, Executor, Administrator, Guardian of any type like for a person or estate, Conservator, Custodian, and any other fiduciary under this Will or otherwise shall qualify and serve without bond, surety, security, surety bond, or similar.

If evidence does not show it likely a person survived me by 120 hours (5 days) then for this Will and my estate they shall be deemed in all ways as having died before me.

If part of this Will is by law invalid or unenforceable other provisions remain in effect.

Any Personal Representative may at any time transfer money or property of a minor under age 18 to a Custodian to act under the North Carolina Uniform Transfers to Minors Act or similar law anywhere, and may pick a person to be Custodian including themselves.

TESTATOR

IN WITNESS WHEREOF, I, __John David Smith__, the Testator, sign my name to this instrument this, and do hereby declare that I sign and execute this instrument as my Will and that I sign it willingly, that I execute it as my free and voluntary act for the purposes therein expressed, and that I am 18 years of age or older, of sound mind, and under no constraint or undue influence.

_____*John David Smith*_____
Signature of Testator

WITNESSES

We, __Mark Elliot Potter__ and __Ann Paula Blom__, the Witnesses, sign our names to this instrument, and do hereby declare that the Testator signs and executes this instrument as the Will of the Testator in our presence and that the Testator signs it willingly, and that each of us at the request of the Testator and in the presence and hearing of the Testator, and in the presence and hearing of each other, hereby signs this Will to function legally as witness to the Testator's signing, and to the best of our knowledge the Testator is eighteen years of age or older, of sound mind, and under no constraint or undue influence.

Mark Elliot Potter	24 Spruce St, Sherwood, NC 27026
Signature of Witness #1	Address of Witness #1
Ann Paula Blom	80 Oak Ave., Edison, North Carolina 27011
Signature of Witness #2	Address of Witness #2

Sample Filled Out Form : Self-Proving Affidavit

SELF-PROVING AFFIDAVIT

(North Carolina General Statutes § 31-11.6)

STATE OF NORTH CAROLINA

COUNTY/CITY OF __MECKLENBURG__

 Before me, the undersigned authority, on this day personally appeared, __John David Smith__, __Mark Elliot Potter__, and __Ann Paula Blom__ known to me to be the Testator and the Witnesses, respectively, whose names are signed to the attached or foregoing instrument and, all of these persons being by me first duly sworn. The Testator, declared to me and to the Witnesses in my presence: That said instrument is the Will of the Testator; that the Testator had willingly signed, and executed it in the presence of said Witnesses as the Testator's free and voluntary act for the purposes therein expressed; or, that the testator signified that the instrument was his instrument by acknowledging to them his signature previously affixed thereto.

The said Witnesses stated before me that the foregoing Will was acknowledged and executed by the Testator as the Will of the Testator in the presence of said Witnesses who, in the presence of the Testator and at the request of Testator, subscribed their names thereto to function as attesting witnesses and that the Testator, at the time of the execution of said will, was over the age of 18 years and of sound and disposing mind and memory.

John David Smith
Testator

Mark Elliot Potter
Witness

Ann Paula Blom
Witness

Subscribed, sworn and acknowledged before me by __John David Smith__, the testator, subscribed and sworn before me by __Mark Elliot Potter__ and __Anna Paula Blom__, witnesses, this __21st__ day of __June__, 20__23__.

(SEAL)   Signature of Notary or Officer: *Janice Fitzgerald*

```
JANICE FITZGERALD
NOTARY PUBLIC
Mecklenburg County
North Carolina
My Commission Expires May 8, 2028
```

www.ingramcontent.com/pod-product-compliance
Lightning Source LLC
Chambersburg PA
CBHW060415220526
45465CB00008B/2897